Fifty Questions on Antisemitism

Who is Jewish?   2 How many Jews are there in the world today?   3 Are Jews nation?   4 Are Jews a race?   5 Can a person have Jewish blood?   6 Are Jews emites?   7 Why do Jews live scattered all over the world?   8 How many Jews nce lived in the Netherlands and how many live there now?   9 Why do so many ews live in the United States?   10 Does a standard definition of antisemitism xist?   11 Where does the word antisemitism come from?   12 Where does the ord Semitic come from?   13 Does Semitism or prosemitism exist?.   14 How old is ntisemitism?   15 What are the most widespread antisemitic myths and legends? 5 Where do economic stereotypes about Jews originate from?   17 Where does e concept of the worldwide Jewish conspiracy come from?   18 What is true out the powerful Jewish lobby in the United States?   19 Are Wall Street and ollywood controlled by Jews?   20 Are all Jews rich?   21 Have Jews and hristians always been each other's enemies?   22 Have Jews and Muslims always een each other's enemies?   23 Did Jews live better in the past under Islam than nder Christianity?   24 Is the New Testament antisemitic?   25 Why have so many hristians seen the Jews as the murderers of Christ?   26 Have Catholics always een more anti-Jewish than Protestants?   27 What does the Koran say about ews?   28 Why have many Jews converted to another religion in the past?   29 Is ere "Islamic antisemitism" nowadays?   30 Has Morocco had a tolerant history ward Jews?   31 Has Turkey had a tolerant history toward Jews?   32 What do e know about the Jews in Surinam?   33 What do we know about the Jews of ruba and the Netherlands Antilles?   34 What is meant by the terms Holocaust d Shoah?   35 How are antisemitism and the Shoah related?   36 Are there fferences between the antisemitic ideas of Hitler and earlier forms of Jew-tred?   37 Did Hitler also despise other so-called Semites?   38 Was the Shoah ique?   39 Is Holocaust denial tolerable?   40 What is Zionism?   41 What is e relationship between Zionism and antisemitism?   42 Is Zionism a form of lonialism?   43 Is Zionism a form of racism?   44 Is the conflict between Israel d the Palestinians a religious conflict?   45 Does Israel treat the Palestinians e same as the Nazis treated the Jews?   46 Is it antisemitic to compare Jews Nazis?   47 Is criticizing Israel antisemitic?   48 How can you tell if antisemitism on the rise?   49 What is meant by the "new" antisemitism?   50 So, what is ally the essence of antisemitism?

Table of Contents

Author & Translator's Note: There is a growing trend among many writers, historians, and (Jewish) organizations in America to adopt the British spelling of antisemitism as the "correct" usage. In this book, we have expressly chosen to support this development by spelling "anti-Semitism" without the hyphen and capital S (see question 13).

Foreword

"Asking questions is a critical activity of living a full life even when the answers are not evident." Elie Wiesel

Antisemitism has not been eliminated. More than sixty years after World War II, there is once again an increase in antisemitism all over the world. The number of violent anti-Jewish incidents is alarmingly high in many European countries. And the perpetrators are not only from right-wing extremist circles. Influenced, in part, by the seemingly hopeless conflict between Israel and the Palestinians, countless Muslim youngsters have translated their solidarity with the Palestinians into a hatred for all things Jewish.

History has taught us that antisemitism is more than just violence against Jews and Jewish institutions. Antisemitism entails a particular state of mind. All sorts of irrational ideas have existed about Jews for centuries: Jews are purportedly out to control the world; they are supposedly spies, usurers, and the murderers of Christ. These and other delusions are still alive and well today, especially – though not exclusively – in the Arab world. Many of these anti-Jewish stereotypes are deeply rooted in European history and are very difficult to eradicate.

By means of questions and answers, this book hopes to provide the reader with insight into the complex phenomenon of antisemitism. This is not a scholarly treatise on antisemitism down through the ages. It is, instead, an attempt to succinctly present a considerable amount of historical material in a straightforward manner. Those questions that are difficult or painful have not been sidestepped. Simple or blatant questions have been tackled as well. The simple questions are often the most difficult to answer. And certainly some of these questions deserve a more in-depth answer than we could provide in a book of this length.

The purpose of *Fifty Questions on Antisemitism* is primarily educational: inviting readers to think for themselves, to ask their own questions, and come up with their own answers. In the long -term, the best way – if not the only way – to fight antisemitism is through education. Another objective of this book is to examine a broad range of opinions. Antisemitism is an issue where people's feelings often run high. The book takes a stance where deemed necessary; it attempts to be discerning where this is possible.

The Anne Frank House is a museum that attracts hundreds of thousands of visitors annually. However, it is much more than just a history museum. The organization itself, which oversees the museum, also develops a countless array of educational activities promoting tolerance and mutual respect in society. It goes without saying that fighting antisemitism is also a part of this. Our organization – as stated in its original statutes – supports the right of the State of Israel to exist. The history of that existence – similar to that of Anne Frank House – is inseparable from the history of anti-semitism. However, this is not meant to suggest that criticizing the politics of the State of Israel is not permitted. Several questions in this book deal with the issue of where the line should be drawn between constructive, acceptable criticism of the politics of Israel and criticism that is simply unacceptable.

A number of illustrations in this book might be perceived as shocking. They have been included here because deplorable images such as these – as well as the deplorable ideas lurking behind them – can only be fought when openly scrutinized.

I hope this book will contribute to more awareness about anti-semitism and its history, and that it will subsequently provide a better footing for answering the question of how present-day antisemitism can be fought.

Hans Westra
Executive Director Anne Frank House

Fifty Questions on Antisemitism

1 thru 9
About Jews and Judaism

Who is Jewish?

Answering the question "Who is Jewish?" goes hand in hand with answering the question "What is Judaism?" Judaism is essentially an age-old religious faith. However, Judaism – similar to Christianity and Islam – is also a cultural tradition. Besides this, many Jews see themselves and other Jews as members of a nation – the Jewish people. The simple question "Who is Jewish?" is more complicated then it appears at first glance, therefore it can be answered in many different ways. According to Jewish tradition, every child born of a Jewish mother is Jewish, as well as anyone who chooses to convert to Judaism following the strict Orthodox Jewish rules and rituals. Remarkable as it might seem, inquiries about someone's religious persuasion are of secondary importance. Somebody with a Jewish mother is always Jewish, whether he or she acts on this or even believes in Judaism. So a person can be Jewish, but at the same time not be very religious. Non-religious Jews are referred to as secular Jews. Many famous people – ranging from the late Albert Einstein to Woody Allen – are secular Jews. In the Netherlands, the majority of Jews are secular and also a large part of the residents of the State of Israel do not consider themselves very religious. Jewish religious tradition also includes different movements. Besides the Orthodox tradition, the most well-known movement is called Liberal Judaism. Though Orthodox Jews hold the upper hand in Israel, the majority of American Jews living in the United States belong to one of many Liberal Jewish communities, for example Reform, Conservative, and Reconstructionist congregations. Liberal Jews tend to answer the question "Who is Jewish?" differently than the Orthodox. According to certain Liberal Jewish traditions, the child of a Jewish father and a non-Jewish mother can also be considered Jewish provided his or her parents declare their intent to raise that child as a Jew. Liberal and Orthodox Jews also disagree about which standards should apply for conversion to Judaism. It is more difficult to become a Jew in Orthodox Jewish tradition because the rules are much stricter. The question of who is and who is not Jewish has also a practical application. According to Israeli law, every single Jew has the right

Orthodox Jewish man, Israel, 1988.

A discotheque in the Israeli city of Arad, 1997.

Young Israelis smoking a water pipe across from the Wailing Wall in Jerusalem, 2004.
The Wailing Wall is on the Temple Mount. The Al-Aska Mosque, also located there,
is a holy place for Muslims.

to request and receive Israeli citizenship (Law of Return). As already pointed out, Orthodox Jews have the upper hand in Israel and in the past their strict rules have always been the ones imposed to answer the question "Who is Jewish?". Yet, there has also been an ongoing discussion on this subject for many years now. Additional regulations continue to be acknowledged and legislated by the Israeli Supreme Court, even as recently as August 2004.

Torah and the Bible

Though Judaism and Christianity are based originally on the same Holy Scriptures, there are differences. The first part of the Hebrew (Jewish) Bible is known as the Torah (also the Five Books of Moses). Orthodox Jewish tradition asserts that God gave the entire Torah to the prophet Moses at Mt. Sinai; it is therefore sacred and indisputable. The Jewish Bible also includes many other Holy Scriptures, such as "The Prophets". In Judaism, the complete Bible is referred to as the Tanach, while Christians call it the Old Testament. Christianity developed directly from Judaism. Christians see Jesus Christ as the Son of God and believe his life, suffering, death and Resurrection were the fulfillment of the Jewish prophecy of the Messiah. However, Judaic tradition does not accept the New Testament – which recounts the life story of Jesus – as part of the Jewish Bible.

The Word Jew

The word Jew can be traced back to *Yehudah* – the Hebrew name of Judah in the Torah – one of the twelve sons of the Jewish patriarch Jacob (renamed Israel – later in the Torah – by an angel of God). Judah and his brothers were the forefathers of one of the Twelve Tribes of Israel. The land they inhabited was divided into a northern Kingdom of Israel and a southern Kingdom of Judah following the death of King Solomon. The Assyrians conquered the Kingdom of Israel and exiled the population in the seventh century B.C.E. marking the beginning of the Diaspora (scattering or dispersion) of the Jewish people (see question 7). In the fifth century B.C.E., the Babylonians conquered the Kingdom of Judah. The descendants of Judah called themselves – and were referred to by others as – *Yehudim* or Jews. The expression Jew appears for the first time in the later books of the Tanach (Old Testament). In earlier books of the Bible, Jews are referred to as "Children of Israel".

02 How many Jews are there in the world today?

The extent of the Jewish population in the world today is, of course, dependent on how one determines who is Jewish. Israeli demographers estimate that around thirteen million Jews live dispersed throughout the entire world. The country with the largest Jewish

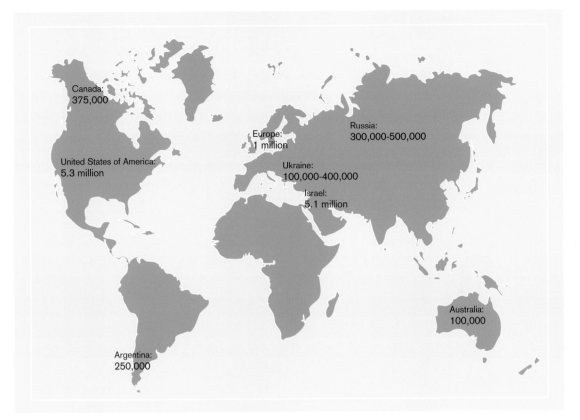

Canada:
375,000

United States of America:
5.3 million

Europe:
1 million

Russia:
300,000-500,000

Ukraine:
100,000-400,000

Israel:
5.1 million

Australia:
100,000

Argentina:
250,000

Before World War II, most of the Jews of the world lived in Europe. Nowadays, the vast majority of Jews live in the United States and Israel.

community (5.3 million) is the United States and almost as many Jews (5.1 million) live in Israel. All together, these communities comprise 80 percent of the total worldwide Jewish population. Only 1.5 million Jews now live in Europe, the part of the world where the most Jews lived before World War II. This last figure is, however, debatable because particularly in the countries of the former Soviet Union (Russia, Ukraine, White Russia) estimates tend to vary from 450,000 to (not less than) 1.3 million Jews. Between 30,000 and 40,000 Jews live in the Netherlands (see question 8). Israeli demographers are alarmed by a number of prevailing trends. The total Jewish population in the world has only increased by two million people since World War II, and in the past thirty years the Jewish population around the world has only grown by 2 percent – in contrast to a 60 percent increase in the total population of the world. This is not only due to a low birth rate among Jews; it is primarily attributable to changing marriage patterns. The percentage of mixed marriages – as well as other forms of partnerships – particularly in the United States and Europe have both increased significantly. More than 50 percent of all American and Dutch Jews marry someone from outside the Jewish community (the percentage of American Jews marrying non-Jews was only 7 percent before World War II) and children from mixed marriages are usually not raised as Jews. These trends seem to indicate that the continuing existence of the Jewish community outside of Israel is threatened and that assimilation – a goal some Jews have struggled to realize for centuries in Europe – has finally occurred.

Additional Figures

France has the largest Jewish population in Western Europe (500,000), but this community is steadily declining. In contrast, Germany has a modest Jewish community (160,000), but one that has grown considerably over the past years due to immigration from Eastern Europe. Between 1970 and 2000, the number of Jews in Israel almost doubled, the Jewish population in Australia increased by almost 50 percent due to immigration and in Latin America by more than 10 percent. The Jewish population in most other countries declined.

03 Are Jews a nation?

The question of whether a group of people thinks of themselves as a nation is best answered by that group itself. For centuries,

Many Orthodox Jews lived in Eastern Europe before World War II. Former Czechoslovakia, 1923.

Jewish woman, Netherlands, 1993.

In Nazi Germany, the so-called Nuremberg Race Laws determined who did and who did not belong to the "Jewish race". This "law for the protection of German blood and German honor", declared on September 15, 1935, distinguished between Germans, half-breeds (of the first and second degree), and Jews. The law also decreed that Germans could no longer marry Jews. Ancestry was the decisive factor in establishing whether somebody was Jewish or German.

no matter where they lived in the world, Jews have considered themselves a part of the same religious family. In Jewish tradition, there have always been references to a Jewish people. Even though being Jewish involves a religious and a historical -cultural component (see question 1), it cannot be defined as a nationality. Jews are found in almost all the countries of the world and most of them boast the nationality of the country where they live. Less than half of the worldwide Jewish population lives in the State of Israel and has Israeli nationality. If a people are defined as "a group of individuals who feel connected to each other by tradition, language, culture, religion, and history" perhaps it is better to speak of Jewish communities instead of "the Jewish people". Jews from the Netherlands speak a different language and have a different history – and partly other cultural and religious traditions – than Jews from Morocco and Turkey. Many people in the past, Jews as well as non-Jews, spoke of the Jewish community as "the Jewish Nation". In this way emphasizing that Jews – similar to people of other European countries – had the right to strive for self-determination. This goal was achieved in 1948 with the establishment of the State of Israel.

Lowercase *j* or Capital *J*?
How should the words Jew and Jewish be written? With a small letter *j* or a capital letter *J*? Both written forms appear in the Dutch language. In Dutch, as well as in English, it is also customary to indicate the name of a country and words that are closely connected using a capital letter: Germany, Spaniard, Greek. Though religious persuasions usually begin with a lowercase letter in Dutch, in English this is exactly the opposite: Christianity, Islam, and Judaism. The word Jewish is used to refer to the religion as well as the people. In many Dutch books published before World War II, the Dutch equivalents of Jews and Jewish were written with a capital *J*. In the Netherlands today, *Nederlandse joden* (Dutch Jews) or *joods* (Jewish) are written using a lowercase *j*. Though this is merely a question of style to some people, for others it is a question of conviction.

04 Are Jews a race?

No, Jews are definitely not a race, because human races do not exist. In terms of biology, there is only one race: the human race. The idea that Jews comprised a separate race was instrumental in the occurrence of the Holocaust. This notion was based on a

theory that Jews the world over had a number of racial characteristics in common; features that had been determined biologically
or genetically and were therefore unvarying. This theory is un-
sound. Racial doctrines and race classification appeared in the
eighteenth century on the heels of the classifications that were
created for plants and animals by the Swedish biologist Linnaeus
(1707-1778). Based on external characteristics such as hair col-
or, hair structure or the shape of a person's nose, all sorts of
classifications were making the rounds then – one even more
far-reaching than the next. Race classification always divided
people into four basic categories: "the White race", "the Yellow
race", "the Black race", and "the Red race". To distinguish the
races from each other, all different human characteristics were
ascribed to people. In addition, a concept of inequality was insti-
tuted right from the start: influential European scientists were
interested in proving the superiority of their own race – the white
race. In Europe, particularly in the nineteenth and first half of the
twentieth century, race classification was very popular. Almost
everybody – rich or poor, conservative or socialist, Christian
or Jew – referred to groups of people as races. This word race
was also frequently used without any inference of bias, meaning
nothing more than sort or blood relationship. Pseudo-scientists
attached a huge amount of significance to race classification.
Scores of personality traits were connected to different races,
which resulted in a variety of bizarre and dangerous ideas. Many
people considered Jews a "pure race", given that they had managed to survive for centuries as a separate group, a "nation
apart". Race classification became very controversial because of
the way in which the Nazis used it in the 1930s and 1940s to distinguish the Aryan from the Semitic race. Following World War II,
scientists conclusively established the irrelevance of race classifications. There is no such thing as a Jew-gene; you cannot
identify "real Jews" by examining their genes.

Race
"Racial beliefs constitute myths about the diversity in the human species and about the abilities and
behavior of people homogenized into 'racial' categories. The myth fused behavior and physical
features together in the public mind, impeding our comprehension of both biological variations and
cultural behavior, implying that both are genetically determined. Racial myths bear no relationship to

the reality of human capacities or behavior. Scientists today find that reliance on such folks' beliefs about human differences in research has lead to countless errors." American Anthropological Association Statement on Race, May 17, 1998.

Classification

"Racial classification is cultural, and it's based on the unfortunate and sad legacy of racial distinction based on this ridiculous metaphor, the purity of blood. You're identifiable as having black ancestry because we can see it. I mean, who's Tiger Wood, who's Colin Powell? Colin Powell is as Irish as he is African, but we don't classify him as that. No, we have a really screwed up classification. To think it's biological is just plain wrong. It's based, flat-out, on the legacy of racism and the metaphor of the purity of the blood. It's a very troubling issue." Stephen Jay Gould (1941-2002), professor of biology at Harvard University, in an interview for the American television network *PBS* (Public Broadcasting System).

05 Can a person have Jewish blood?

No, there is no such thing as Jewish blood. However, the notion that a person's blood somehow determines his or her character is deeply rooted in European history. Today we know better: genes in combination with upbringing determine the character and personality of every individual – not the blood that runs through somebody's veins. The search for "Jewish blood" has resulted in the large-scale expulsion and murder of Jews on at least two occasions in history. In fifteenth century Spain, the doctrine of "purity of blood" (*limpieza de sangre*) was a powerful weapon used against so-called Conversos – Jews who converted to Christianity – that is "new" Christians. Christians with "Jewish blood" in their veins ran the risk of being persecuted by the Inquisition. The struggle for power between old and new Christians ended in 1492 with the expulsion of all the Jews from Spain, and then from Portugal. Four-hundred-and-fifty years later, the National Socialists (Nazis) in Germany were just as convinced that everyone with "Jewish blood" was a threat to society. A notorious blood test conducted at the Berlin *Institut für Rassenforschung* (Institute for Racial Study) was one of the methods used to determine if somebody actually had Jewish blood. Remarkably, the investigations done by this institution indicated a much greater relationship between Jewish and non-Jewish Germans than between German and French Jews. Unfortunately, not even this deterred the Nazis from persecuting the Jews of Germany and France.

The Nuremberg Race Laws
The Race Laws decreed by the National Socialists in 1935, also known as the Nuremberg Laws, were meant to protect "German blood". A marriage or relationship between a German and someone with Jewish or "mixed blood" was forbidden. To determine if someone had Jewish or German blood, the religious affiliation of his or her grandparents would usually be ascertained. Most of Germany's churches willingly cooperated with this official registration.

06 Are Jews Semites?

The fact that hatred directed against Jews is called antisemitism (see questions 10 through 20) does not mean that Jews are Semites. The question is not so much "Are Jews Semites?" but "Do Semites actually exist?" Semitic is a linguistic concept, denoting a number of related languages. Hebrew and Arabic are included in the Semitic language group, as well as Maltese, a language spoken on the Island of Malta. Maltese is the only European Semitic language. However, the languages that many Jews in Europe used to speak – Yiddish, for example, and Ladino – a language originally spoken by many Jews in the countries around the Mediterranean Sea – are not Semitic languages. These languages belong to the Indo-European group. Those who regard Semites as ethnically related groups of people tend to run into problems. A huge amount of ethnic diversity already exists among people who only speak an Arabic language. Equating people with language – or language with ethnicity – has been one of the huge blunders of science over the past two hundred years. The confusion more or less continues up until the present-day. One sometimes hears the comment that Arabs cannot be antisemites because they themselves are Semites. A flawed rationale, given that people who speak a language related to Hebrew can certainly be anti-Jewish. The Dutch can also be anti-German and Germans can despise the Dutch, regardless of the fact that Dutch and German are languages that are closely related.

The most important Semitic languages are Arabic, Hebrew, and Aramaic. Dialects of Aramaic are still spoken in Southeastern Turkey, Northern Iraq, and Western Iran. Berber is considered a Hamitic language and Turkish belongs to the family of Altaic languages.

The destruction of the second Temple of Jerusalem in the year 70 C.E. was a major event in the history of the Jewish Diaspora. This seventeenth century rendering, by French painter Nicolas Poussin, shows Roman soldiers setting the temple afire. For background information, Poussin consulted a description of the incident by the Jewish historian Flavius Josephus (37 C.E. – circa 100 C.E.). Josephus writes in his book the *Jewish War* that Roman soldiers, much to the displeasure of the Roman General Titus, accidentally set the temple afire.

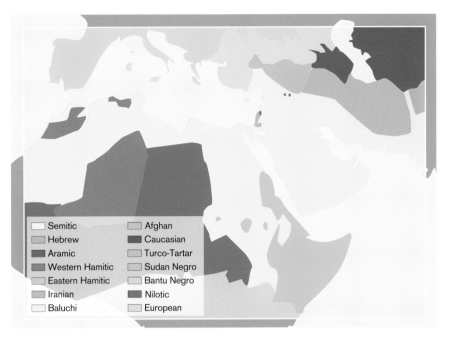

- Semitic
- Hebrew
- Aramic
- Western Hamitic
- Eastern Hamitic
- Iranian
- Baluchi
- Afghan
- Caucasian
- Turco-Tartar
- Sudan Negro
- Bantu Negro
- Nilotic
- European

07 Why do Jews live scattered all over the world?

Jewish history has been a history of wanderings. The first books of the Bible tell the story of the Jews who were slaves in Egypt. After rising up against the Egyptians, they wandered for many years in the desert – the period of Exodus from Egypt – to finally settle in what is now known as Israel. Many years later, in the seventh century B.C.E., the Assyrians conquered a large part of that country and much of the population was carried off as slaves. There has been much speculation as to their fate. In the year 586 B.C.E., the Babylonians conquered Jerusalem and destroyed the Holy Temple of the Jewish people, which had been built by King Solomon. A large part of the population was again carried off as slaves, now to Babylon (a city that was located in present-day Iraq south of Baghdad). The Jews were finally allowed to return home seventy years later when the Persian king, Cyrus the Great, defeated Babylon. Some of them chose to settle instead in Egypt or on the Arabian Peninsula. Many Jews specialized in trading. In the year 70 C.E., the second Holy Temple of Jerusalem was destroyed. The Roman occupying force ousted the Jews who rebelled against them from the city and the country. Large groups of Jewish prisoners were carried off to Rome; many other Jews fled to cities in Turkey and Greece. In the early centuries of the Christian Era, a considerable Jewish community had also already settled in Spain. The Roman Emperor Constantine proclaimed Christianity the state religion of his empire at the beginning of the fourth century. From that moment on, the Christian religion overtook its "competitor" and predecessor Judaism. Due to the Arab conquests of the seventh century, the rise of Islam, and various Crusades in the thirteenth century, only a few thousand Jews still lived in what is now known as Israel. There were, however, Jewish communities all over Europe and the Middle East and every harbor city had its share of Jewish traders.

The Diaspora (dispersion or scattering) of the Jews is more or less a story of (forced) migration and of trade. This forced migration was often the result of conflicts and wars and unfortunately is not unique. The history of Europe, the Middle East and the Mediterranean region tells a bloody story, and tolerance for ethnic and religious minorities was often lacking. Many minorities were assimilated, exterminated, or otherwise disappeared during the course of history. After more than two thousand years, it is exceptional that Jews have not completely "disappeared" or been assimilated and that they live scattered across so many different countries. It is estimated that there were eight to ten million Jews in the world during the time of the Roman Empire. If one compares the population increases among other groups, there should now be approximately two hundred million Jews. Yet, presently there are only thirteen million Jews (see question 2) living throughout the world. This discrepancy can be attributed to expulsion and murder, conversion to Christianity and Islam, and assimilation.

08 How many Jews once lived in the Netherlands and how many live there now?

Anywhere from 30,000 to 40,000 Jews live in the Netherlands today. Approximately a quarter of them have Israeli nationality; the rest are of course Dutch; and there is also a modest community of Jews from abroad (exact figures are not readily available). The

About Jews and Judaism

Before World War II, the Jewish neighborhood of Amsterdam stretched from the Nieuwmarkt in the old city center to the Weesperplein, a square on the Amstel River. The Sunday market on the Jodenbreestraat and Uilenburgerstraat were always crowded with shoppers. In Amsterdam nowadays, the flea market on the Waterlooplein is merely a reminder of the many pre-war Jewish marketplaces that bustled with activity. (also photo previous page)

Jewish population of the Netherlands was considerably larger before World War II, consisting of around 140,000 individuals. More than 100,000 of them did not survive the Nazi Occupation. Amsterdam was the center of Dutch Jewish life before the war. There was a large Jewish neighborhood situated in the center of the old city surrounding two squares – Nieuwmarkt and Waterlooplein. This area was especially known for its lively markets. Many working-class Jewish families lived there crammed into small apartments. The history of Amsterdam's Jews began with the arrival of Portuguese traders at the end of the sixteenth century. They were the direct descendants of Jews who had been expelled from Spain and Portugal and were granted permission by the city council to settle in Amsterdam. They mainly traded in sugar, coffee, wood and tobacco from Brazil and diamonds and cotton from the Dutch East Indies. Much of Amsterdam's growth and prosperity in the seventeenth century and its status as a center of world trade can be attributed, for a large degree, to this group of merchants. They were called Portuguese Jews because they spoke to each other in the Portuguese language.

Jews from Middle and Eastern Europe began arriving in Amsterdam in 1630. These Jews, who had fled war-related violence and persecution in Germany and Poland, spoke Yiddish and were referred to as High German Jews. In comparison to other places, there was a relatively high degree of religious tolerance in the Netherlands – then known as the (Dutch) Republic of the Seven Provinces. Though the Jews in Amsterdam were tolerated as a minority, this did not mean there was absolutely no discrimination. Jews were finally allowed to build a synagogue that was visible from the street in the middle of the seventeenth century. The construction of the Portuguese Synagogue located on today's Mr. Visserplein and the building of the *Grote Sjoel* (The Great Synagogue) of the High-German Jewish community located on today's Jonas Daniël Meijerplein were both begun in 1670. The Great Synagogue, where Amsterdam's Jewish Historical Museum has been located since 1987, opened to worshippers in 1671. The Portuguese *Snoge*, still in use as a synagogue today, was completed in 1675. In the eighteenth century, Jews settled in various places outside Amsterdam. So, besides *Mokum* – a Yiddish

word that means place and specifically refers to Amsterdam –
a *Mediene*, Yiddish for surrounding or countryside, was established as well. All of the Jewish communities outside of Amsterdam
belonged to the *Mediene*. The Jews in the Netherlands had been
granted civil rights as a direct result of the French Revolution at
the end of the eighteenth century, They were then allowed to settle
anywhere in the country. However, Amsterdam remained the center of Jewish life in the Netherlands. By the beginning of World
War II approximately 10 percent of the population of Amsterdam
was Jewish. For a brief period during the German Occupation,
the Jewish neighborhood was surrounded by fences and barbed
wire – transformed for the first time in its history into an actual
ghetto. What was left of Amsterdam's Jewish neighborhood when
the war ended was a painful reminder in the heart of the city.

Ashkenazi and Sephardic Jews
The culture of the generally well-to-do Portuguese Jewish traders differed greatly from that of the
penniless High-German Jewish refugees. The two groups spoke different languages and with regard
to social, economic, and cultural affairs formed two distinct communities. Jews of Spanish-Portuguese
decent are also called Sephardic Jews (*Sephardim*); Jews from Germany and Eastern Europe are
referred to as Ashkenazi Jews (*Ashkenazim*). However, their common religion was what mattered most
to the Dutch; they were seen as one group.

Baruch de Spinoza (1632-1677).
Print: Jean Charles Francois.

Spinoza
Baruch de Spinoza (1632-1677) was one of the most famous Jews to have lived in the Netherlands.
The son of a Portuguese Jewish trader, he became a philosopher of international renown. He grew
up amidst the ambience of Jewish Amsterdam. In 1656, he was driven from the Portuguese Jewish
community because he rejected all forms of dogmatic religion in his statements and writings.
He pleaded for complete religious tolerance and became one of the most important forerunners of the
Enlightenment. The philosophy of Spinoza was characterized by rational thinking. His new interpretation
of God was individualistic and he undeservedly acquired the reputation of being an atheist.

09 Why do so many Jews live in the United States?

Approximately 5.3 million Jews live in the United States of America.
Among a population of more than 280 million people, they account

At the end of the 1800s and beginning of the 1900s, the Lower Eastside – a neighborhood in downtown Manhattan (New York City) – was the first place many Jewish immigrants settled in America. The mass emigration of poor and persecuted Eastern European Jews to the United States became one of the great success stories of Jewish and American history. This photograph was taken around the turn of the century.

A Russian Jewish immigrant on Ellis Island, an island at the mouth of the Hudson River in New York harbor where immigrants wanting to enter the United States were first screened. This photo was taken in 1900 during the great wave of immigration to America. A U.S. Customs Office and the Immigration Museum are located on Ellis Island today.

for roughly 2 percent of the total. Although the largest Jewish community in the world lives in this country, they are still a small minority. In comparison, 85 percent of Americans are Christian – two out of three are Protestant and 30 percent are Catholic. Though it is more difficult to determine the number of Muslims in the United States, because many are not affiliated with a mosque, their numbers are estimated at five to six million. The number of Jews in America is partially dependent on how a count is carried out. The majority of American Jews are affiliated with one of many Liberal Jewish communities and Liberal Judaism is more lenient in defining who is and who is not Jewish (see question 1). Three out of every ten Jews in the United States are married to someone with a different religious belief, usually Christian. In the past few years, the percentage of mixed marriages has even exceeded 50 percent. The Orthodox Jewish community in America is seriously concerned that this will contribute to a further watering down of Jewish culture and tradition. America primarily owes its substantial Jewish population to the large-scale European Jewish migration that peaked between 1880 and 1920. During these decades, the number of Jews in the United States increased from approximately 230,000 (1880) to 3.5 million (1920). America was then the pre-eminent country of immigration and a huge amount of Eastern-European Jews, plagued by poverty and pogroms, boarded ships to take them to America's shores. In the 1920s, the American government established a quota for immigrant groups and though Eastern-European Jews were still admitted, their numbers were limited. The story of the Jewish immigration to America is one of the great success stories of Jewish (and American) history. In two or three generations, the majority of these immigrants managed to work their way out of poverty to become relatively well-to-do average Americans.

Pogroms

The term pogrom is derived from Russian. It can be defined as an organized brawl frequently accompanied by plundering and murder. There were a number of extremely bloody pogroms in Russia specifically directed at the Jews at the end of the nineteenth century. However, it was primarily the pogroms that took place in the villages and cities in the year 1881 that led scores of Russian Jews to seek refuge elsewhere. Many of them saw the United States as a "promised land". In the nineteenth century, a few million Jews lived in the western part of Russia – the only region of the country where they had been allowed to settle. Pogroms against Jews had also occurred in the Middle Ages, particularly in Germany.

An Orthodox Jewish woman and her children in Brooklyn (New York), 1995.

About Jews and Judaism

Four hundred Jews died during the 1905 pogrom in the Russian city of Odessa (in the Crimea). Some of the bodies of those murdered Jews are lined up in a row in this photo. In spite of antisemitism, pogroms, and emigration, Odessa was an important cultural center for the Jews living in the southern part of Russia up until the Communist period, which began in 1917.

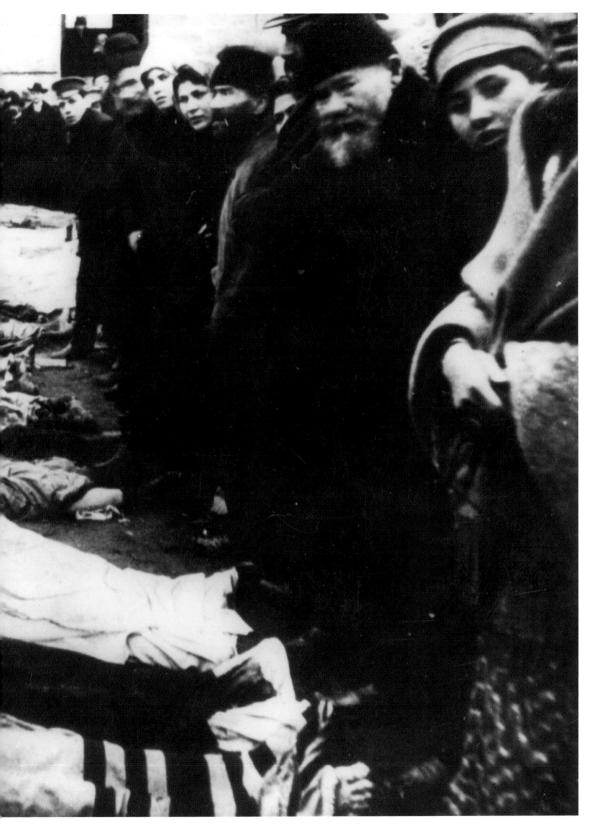

Fifty Questions on Antisemitism

10 thru 20
About the History
of Antisemitism

10 Does a standard definition of antisemitism exist?

In the vernacular, antisemitism is generally a synonym for the hatred of Jews. The adjective antisemitic is often used to mean anti-Jewish. However, a standard definition of this concept – what is included or for that matter excluded – does not exist. In numerous books, the concept antisemitism is used to define a wide range of negative attitudes toward Jews throughout the ages: from ethnic conflicts in ancient times, to religious rivalry and economic exclusion in the Middle Ages, on to pogroms of the nineteenth century and the far-reaching mass murders of the twentieth century. There are huge differences of opinion among scholars as to whether all these phenomena can be classified under the single denominator of antisemitism. Many argue that antisemitism is too broad a concept, indiscriminately covering all kinds of Jew-hatred no matter where or when it occurred. Therefore, in order to have a good historical understanding, it is essential to differentiate. A three-part breakdown that is regularly used is the distinction between religious antisemitism (also referred to as anti-Judaism); social-economic antisemitism (the exclusion of Jews from certain professions, particularly in the Middle Ages); and the political antisemitism that arose in the nineteenth century primarily based on racial doctrines (see question 11). This problem related to usage has existed since the concept antisemitism was first introduced. The word was conceived as an alternative or even as the successor to the concept anti-Judaism – an aversion to Judaism as a religion. A strong tradition of anti-Judaism was set in motion in ancient times and continued into the Middle Ages, particularly within the Christian Church. At the end of the nineteenth century, many people considered antisemitic ideas "modern". Antisemitism was no longer based on the familiar "old-fashioned" religious

A postcard from Germany (1900) depicting a Jewish woman (Susanna) as filthy and obese. Anti-Jewish postcards were all the rage in Europe a hundred years ago.

A Jewish immigrant from Eastern Europe speaking in a thick Yiddish accent tries to sell an Englishman a sponge used for bathing babies. If the customer does not have a baby of his own, then the peddler suggests he would be more than willing to lend out one of his many. A postcard from 1913.

A French election poster from 1889. Adolf Willette openly presents himself as antisemitic in his bid for a seat in the Parliament: "Jews are another race and our enemy," is clearly displayed on the poster.

prejudices, but on "new", seemingly scientific, racial doctrines. Both religious and racist antisemitic ideas continue to surface today.

11 Where does the word antisemitism come from?

Wilhelm Marr (1819-1904) is considered the father of antisemitism.

The word antisemitism became popular around 1880 because of articles and pamphlets written by Wilhelm Marr, a German journalist. Marr coined this new term to express his aversion to Jews and to gain supporters for his League of Antisemites. Even though Marr himself was not the originator of the word – who was remains a mystery – he has been consigned to posterity as the "father of antisemitism". So, the concept of antisemitism was popularized by an antisemite. With the introduction of this word, Marr joined the ranks of many contemporary scholars of his time. At the end of the eighteenth century, linguists began looking at ways in which different languages were related to each other.

Marr's book *Der Sieg des Juden-thums über das Germanenthum* (The Triumph of Judaism over Germanism), published in the later part of the nineteenth century, was reissued in no less than twelve reprints within a very brief period.

Semitic languages are an example of one of these groups of related languages. Hebrew, Arabic, Aramaic all fall under the Semitic language group, as well as a few other languages that were no longer spoken, so-called dead languages. Languages are also distinguished into Indo-European and Turkish language groups. According to race classification of the nineteenth century, those who spoke a Semitic language belonged to the so-called Semitic race. They were designated Semites. Many native German-speakers of that time saw themselves as Germanic members of the so-called Aryan race. The belief that there were fundamental differences between Aryans and Semites (later called the Aryan myth) was a focal point of Wilhelm Marr's ideas. Equating language, people, and race was very common in those days. For Marr, the concept "antisemitism" only concerned Jews and his campaign was directed against them. His antisemitic texts appeared at a time when many others also took up the pen in reaction to the emancipation of Germany's Jews. In 1871, the newly established unified German State had granted Jews equal rights as citizens.

Inconceivable

Wilhelm Marr's book *Der Sieg des Judenthums über das Germanenthum* (The Triumph of Judaism over Germanism) was published in 1879 and reissued in no less than twelve reprints within a very brief period. It has been described as the "first antisemitic bestseller." As inconceivable as it might sound, Marr had many Jewish friends and was married three times to Jewish women! At the end of his life, he broke with the movement – turning away from antisemitism – and asked the Jews for forgiveness for what he had written.

12 Where does the word Semitic come from?

The adjective Semitic signifies Shem, one of the three sons of Noah. In Genesis, the first book of the Bible, Noah is described as one of the forefathers of the human race. Genesis 6-9 tells how the "corrupt" earth was completely covered in water by

In the Bible, Genesis 9 recounts the tale of Noah: while in a state of drunken unconsciousness, his sons Shem and Japheth cover him with a cloak to hide their father's nakedness. The Italian artist Michelangelo (1475-1564) depicted this and other Bible stories on the walls of the Sistine Chapel. These famous frescos, located in the Vatican, were painted in the period 1508-1512.

"the Flood". Nevertheless, righteous Noah and his family were spared. Forewarned by God, he built an ark in which his family and the animals (seven pairs from the clean animals, and one pair from the unclean) could survive. After the Flood, God made a covenant with Noah never to destroy the earth again; the rainbow was the sign of this promise. Noah's three sons were named Shem, Ham and Japheth. The last is traditionally recognized as the forefather of the Indo-European people; Shem is seen as the forefather of the Semites – the "People of the Book" – the Chosen People. Shem was granted this privilege because of the respect he showed to his father at a moment when his father was drunk. In contrast, Ham – the forefather of the people of Africa – was cursed by his father because he did not display this same degree of respect. This story was used for ages to legitimize the enslavement of Africans; supposedly, their "inferiority" had been laid down in the Tanach – or Old Testament. In early Christian and Jewish circles – and to a lesser extent in the Islamic world – much credence has been given to the notion that all the

nations of the world are descended from one of Noah's three sons. However, there is an abundance of historical, linguistic, archeological and ethnographic evidence that the "Table of Nations" (a detailed listing of the descendants of the three sons of Noah) found in the Bible (Genesis 10) is a mythical account. There has been a great deal of misunderstanding created in the last two hundred years based on the theory that people who speak the same or a similar language are somehow related to each other racially (see question 6).

The Three Sons of Noah

"The sons of Noah who came out of the ark were Shem, Ham and Japheth. (Ham was the father of Canaan.) These were the three sons of Noah, and from them came the people who were scattered over the earth. Noah, a man of the soil, proceeded to plant a vineyard. When he drank some of its wine, he became drunk and lay uncovered inside his tent. Ham, the father of Canaan, saw his father's nakedness and told his two brothers outside. But Shem and Japheth took a garment and laid it across their shoulders; then they walked in backward and covered their father's nakedness. Their faces were turned the other way so that they would not see their father's nakedness. When Noah awoke from his wine and found out what his youngest son had done to him, he said, 'Cursed be Canaan! The lowest of slaves will he be to his brothers.' He also said, 'Blessed be the LORD, the God of Shem! May Canaan be the slave of Shem. May God extend the territory of Japheth; may Japheth live in the tents of Shem, and may Canaan be his slave.' After the Flood Noah lived 350 years. Altogether, Noah lived 950 years, and then he died." NIV Bible (New International Version), Genesis 9:18-29.

13 Does Semitism or prosemitism exist?

Benjamin Disraeli (1804-1881) was the Prime Minister of Great Britain in 1868 and served again from 1874 to 1878. Disraeli was Jewish by birth but converted to Christianity. Nevertheless, he glorified "the Jewish race" in the novels he wrote.

The phenomenon Semitism, in itself, does not exist. Antisemitism is derived from the adjective Semitic, which designates a group of related languages. Antisemitism is therefore not directed, as the word might suggest, against Semitism. The term was conceived to describe an anti-Jewish movement and anti-Jewish ideas. Prosemitism does not exist either. Now and then, the concept philosemitism is used as the opposite of antisemitism. However, this term also carries its negative connotations: a philosemite can be someone with an exaggerated love of Jews or somebody who believes in the "superiority" of Jews. For example, the nineteenth century British Prime Minister Benjamin Disraeli – who was Jewish by birth but converted to Christianity – has gone down in history as a philosemite. In his novels and other works, he glorified "the Jewish race". The term philosemite was used in a negative fashion at the end nineteenth century in reference to the Dreyfus affair in France (see question 15) and pogroms in Russia. People who rejected antisemitism or objected to the violent persecution of Jews were accused of being "Jew-lovers" or "philosemites".

With or without a hyphen?

Not only is there much disagreement about what the concept antisemitism should actually include, there is also disagreement about how the word itself should be spelled. In the Netherlands, for example, some people write the Dutch word *anti-semitisme* with a hyphen, but not very often. The word usually appears in American publications spelled with a hyphen and a capital letter *S*: anti-Semitism. While in British English, it is spelled as one word with a lowercase *s*: antisemitism. Is this so important, does the hyphen actually make any difference? Yes, absolutely. Using a hyphen in the spelling is more than just a linguistic or grammatical question. Including the hyphen more or less implies that the words Semitism or Semite are meaningful in themselves. Not true – because Semites and Semitism do not really exist – and how can you be "anti" something that is nonexistent? This is also the reason that some people in the United States choose to break with the accepted American spelling and write it instead as one word: antisemitism. In addition, many writers, historians, and (Jewish) organizations in America have adopted the British spelling of antisemitism as the "correct" usage. In this book, we have expressly chosen to support this development and have spelled "anti-Semitism" without the hyphen and capital *S*.

14 How old is antisemitism?

Antisemitism is often called "the oldest form of hatred". However, the question of just how old is extremely dependent on how the concept is defined (see question 10). As a relatively new concept, antisemitism is often used to describe – in retrospect as well – many rather diverse forms of Jew-hatred and rivalry between Jews and non-Jews. Several overview works on the history of antisemitism begin with the period of Greek rule, at the time of the conquests of Alexander the Great (332 B.C.E.). During Grecian times and partly in the Roman period that followed, Jews lived in what was then called Palestine and as a religious minority in a number of areas around the Mediterranean Sea and throughout the Middle East. Diverse anti-Jewish texts from this period do exist and there

The reign of Alfons X the Wise (1221-1284) was a high point in Spanish history. A beautifully illustrated songbook from that period: *Las Cantigas de Santa Maria* (The Songs of St. Maria) is testimony to this even today. This work contains miracles attributed to Mary in song form. In the tales that the songs tell, the Virgin Mary protects nonbelievers – such as Jews and Moors – in the same manner that Alfons protected them. Jews can be recognized in the illustrations in this songbook by the type of hat they are wearing – the Jew hat.

In Frankfurt Germany, the Jews lived in Judengasse (Jew Alley), which was plundered in the year 1614. Here, the Jews being driven from the city after this plundering.

About the History of Antisemitism

The Codex Manesse is the most comprehensive and famous German songbook of the Middle Ages. Only one Jew appears in the richly illustrated Codex, Susskind von Trimberg. His outfit includes a blue cloak with a fur collar finished by a gold-colored Jew hat. The Codex was compiled in the second half of the thirteenth century.

The Lambeth Bible, possibly from Canterbury and written in the twelfth century, contains many illustrations of the Old Testament scriptures. This illustration depicts the story of Moses and the Ark of the Covenant (from the Book of Numbers). In this particular Bible, Jews are usually drawn wearing the Jew hat. In 1290, all the Jews were expelled from England.

The entrance to the Jewish ghetto of the Italian city of Venice. The ghetto was established in 1516, when the Venetian city council made it mandatory for Jewish merchants and bankers to live in this secluded city neighborhood. Many other European cities followed the Venetian example and set-up ghettos for their Jewish residents. When Napoleon gained control of Venice (1797), the ghetto was officially disbanded.

The form of the Jew hat as dictated by the local authority of the German city of Frankfurt. This etching dates from the fifteenth century.

were even pogroms against Jews. The most notorious pogrom was the murder of the Jews in the Egyptian city of Alexandria (66 C.E.). Other historians prefer to place the emphasis on antisemitism in the Middle Ages, for example at the time of the Crusades – a period when Jews were expelled from many European countries – or to emphasize antisemitism during the height of the Inquisition, which occurred later on. At that time, religiously inspired anti-Jewish myths and accusations took on grotesque forms (see question 15). The second half of the Middle Ages was also the time when economic life in many European countries was organized around guilds. Guilds were closed associations of merchants and artisans. In order to practice certain professions, membership in a guild was required. Only Christians could join a guild; Jews were excluded from becoming members. The only occupations Jews were allowed to practice were "new" professions such as trading (often only in secondhand merchandise) and lending money with interest. The Church forbade the latter for Christians. This caused economically tinted stereotypes about Jews to arise (see question 16). The granting of equal rights and the emancipation of the Jews in Europe began with the French Revolution at the end of the eighteenth century. Almost all the Jewish ghettos in Europe were officially disbanded in the first half of the nineteenth century. Jews were granted equal rights as citizens and the guilds and universities became accessible to them. Despite the emancipation of Jews in European society – and partly due to it – politically and racially motivated antisemitism gained in popularity and influence in the second half of the nineteenth century (see question 11).

Ghettos

A ghetto was an isolated city neighborhood where Jews were once forced to live. European Jews, however, lived in separate neighborhoods long before the existence of ghettos. In many harbors and trading cities, Jews or other minorities chose to live together in their own groups. Isolated, walled-off ghettos for Jews were created in the Middle Ages. Several popes and many Church Officials encouraged the physical separation of Christians and Jews. The Jewish ghetto of Rome – which existed longer than all the others – was finally torn down in 1870. The word ghetto is derived from the Italian word *gettare*, which means to cast. At the beginning of the sixteenth century, the Jews of Venice were forced to live in the foundry neighborhood where cannons for ships were cast. In the Muslim world, Jews sometimes chose to live in separate neighborhoods for their own safety. The Jewish quarters of Morocco – the Mellahs – are well-known. Though forced resettlement and the isolation of Jews sometimes occurred in the Muslim world, this was not commonplace.

Jew Hat
In the second half of the Middle Ages, Jews had to wear certain kinds of clothing. The Pope and his bishops decided in the year 1215 that Jews should be distinguished from Christians by their attire. Though every city had its own dress code, the common identifying emblems were a yellow spot or a yellow circle resembling a ring on the chest and a pointed hat – the Jew hat. This stigmatizing clothing can still be seen in many of the etchings and paintings from this period.

15 What are the most widespread antisemitic myths and legends?

Scores of the myths and legends concerning Jews can be traced back to the Middle Ages. These legends were responsible for the large-scale persecution and expulsion of the Jews in countless European countries. The "modern times" – starting with the nineteenth century when antisemitism acquired a more political character – contributed as well to the creation of obscure tales about Jews. Some of these legends continue to reappear in the twenty-first century. The most malicious myth of all time is the one that accuses the Jews of murdering Christ (see question 25). In the Middle Ages, an entire series of religiously-inspired myths evolved directly out of this idea. Jews were supposedly guilty of ritually sacrificing (blood libel myth) Christian children. The blood of these children was allegedly used to prepare the matzahs (also matzos or unleavened bread) eaten during the Jewish holiday of Passover. Jews have also been accused on numerous occasions of the desecration of the Host. These consecrated wafers (seen by Catholics as the body of Christ) were allegedly stabbed with knives, thus murdering Jesus all over again. Myths about the Jew as conspirator are also archetypal. These legends have their roots in the Middle Ages too. All sorts of stories in which Jews tried to

A page of the famous Evangeliarium of Heinrich des Löwen
(Henry the Lion), Duke of Bavaria
& Saxony, circa 1130-1195.
An Evangeliarium is a booklet
containing the four Gospels of the
New Testament. Henry the Lion's
Evangeliarium has a gold cover
and contains gorgeous illustrations. The apostles and Jesus have
halos; the (unbelieving) Jews are
wearing the Jew hat.

Jews desecrating the Host, which
bleeds accordingly. This illustration
is from the Lovell Lectionary, an
elaborately illustrated manuscript
from the fifteenth century. Even
though no Jews lived in England at
that time, antisemitic stereotypes
still existed.

This illustration from the Hortus
Deliciarum (Garden of Delights)
depicts the Jews burning in Hell
(middle, left). The Hortus Deliciarum was an illustrated encyclopedia from the twelfth century. The
original book was destroyed by fire
in Strasbourg in 1870. A facsimile
of the Hortus Deliciarum was created based on copies of the book
and annotations. It appeared in
1979.

"The Day of Judgment" is a French
mystery play (medieval religious
drama based on Scriptures and
related to the life of Christ) from
the fourteenth century. The Antichrist (the Devil) – who triumphs
over the Jews, kings and cardinals
– is the central figure of the story.
However, with the Pope at the
helm, the Antichrist is defeated.
Three Jewish followers of the Devil
are depicted here wearing the Jew
hat.

The stained glass windows of the
Gothic-style Saint Michael Cathedral in Brussels portray the Jews
desecrating the Host. Using daggers, the Jews are stabbing the
holy wafer (for Catholics the body
of Christ) so it begins to bleed.

The Jewish Army Captain Dreyfus
– whose image appears in this
poster as "the Traitor!" – was un-
justly accused of treason in France
in 1894. Convicted and sentenced
to life, he was deported to the
prison camp on Devil's Island. He
was finally rehabilitated in 1906.
Jews were often (and still are)
depicted as snakes in antisemitic
posters.

The Profanation of the Host depicted on six panels by the Italian Renaissance painter Paolo Uccello. The panels were originally created for the altarpiece of the Corpus Domini Church in the Italian city of Urbino. They were painted in the middle of the fifteenth century and hang today in the museum of the Ducal Palace in Urbino. Panel 1: A woman sells the holy wafer (Host) to a Jewish merchant. Panel 2: When the merchant tries to burn the wafer, it begins to bleed. The merchant is arrested. Panel 3: Church officials bless the Host once again. Panel 4: The woman who sold the Host is punished. An angel descends from heaven. Panel 5: The Jewish merchant and his family are burned at the stake. Panel 6: Two angels and two devils battle for the soul of the woman.

enslave Christians were commonplace in those days, as well as stories about Jews who conspired with heretics or lepers. Beginning with the Renaissance, conspiracy myths were frequently used for political gain – particularly in Spain. Jews in nineteenth century France and Germany – often closely associated with Freemasons – were accused in countless publications of trying to undermine traditional Christian order. The notorious *Protocols of the Elders of Zion* (see question 17) are based on French texts from this period. Jews have not only been blamed for the French Revolution (1789) but for the Communist Revolution in Russia (1917) as well. A third recurring theme is that of the Jew as traitor. In countless theological texts, the Jews are associated with Judas, originally a disciple and later the betrayer of Jesus Christ. This legend of the Jew as traitor has appeared in different guises: Jews supposedly collaborated with the Ottoman armies that invaded Christian Europe in the sixteenth century. It was also alleged that the Jews subversively worked as a fifth column for the invading Tatars, who were believed to be the Ten Lost Tribes of Israel coming to avenge their oppressed brethren. This betrayal theme also reappears again in the nineteenth century during the Dreyfus Affair. At that time, an army captain named Alfred Dreyfus, a French Jew, was accused of passing military secrets to the Germans. France was gripped by this affair for years. The Jews in Germany were blamed decades later for that country's defeat in World War I. Supposedly Jews were directly responsible for the German Army being "stabbed in the back".

Bloody Folktales

Throughout the centuries, mixing images of Jews and blood has repeatedly proven to be the perfect ingredients for the creation of anti-Jewish myths that have gone done in history as blood libel myths. The legend of the desecration of the Host has cropped up in a myriad of places in Europe. In Brussels in the year 1370, the Hosts supposedly began to bleed after Jews, brandishing knives and daggers, stabbed them to express their hatred of the Christian religion. The small Jewish community of Brussels did not survive this incident; the Jews were murdered or banished. Today, the stained glass windows of the stunning Saint Michael Cathedral in Brussels still portray the entire tale. According to another blood libel myth, Jews needed Christian blood in order to cure themselves of skin diseases. The so-called reason so many Jews suffered from these illnesses was due to their greatest crime, the Crucifixion of Christ. Therefore, Jews allegedly preferred murdering babies with "pure" blood – innocents who were still touched by the "magic of baptism".

Bestseller

In present-day Syria, the book *Matzah of Zion* written by Minister of Defense Mustafa Tlass has been on the bestseller list for twenty years. In this book, Jews are accused of killing small children so they can use their blood in the preparation of matzahs. In 2003, the Arabic satellite-sender *Al Manar*, the station of Hezbollah, broadcast a thirty-episode television series about the "criminal history of Zionism." Jews were depicted, here as well, performing the ritual murders of children so they could use their blood to make matzahs. Antisemitic myths that originated in the Middle Ages are still being widely circulated today.

A Jewish invention?
The belief that Communism was a "Jewish invention" has gained substantial ground in the last century, especially in Eastern Europe. This myth has significantly contributed to the already existing anti-Jewish feelings in these countries. It is true that the Communist movement in the first decades of the twentieth century appealed to large groups of Jewish workers, especially in Russia. They saw Communism as a doctrine of salvation; an immense step forward compared to the politically backward Czarist Empire with its anti-Jewish pogroms and the Jew-hatred stirred up by the Russian Orthodox Church. Initially, Russia's Bolshevik movement was also supported by a group of Jewish artists and intellectuals. However, right after the Bolsheviks took control, the revolution in Russia turned on the Jews. Jewish institutions were disbanded, Hebrew was labeled as a reactionary language and forbidden, and Zionists were persecuted. Stalin launched intensive campaigns against Jews both before and after World War II. Nonetheless, in the former East Bloc countries, there is still much credence attached to the legend that Communism was a Jewish invention.

16 Where do economic stereotypes about Jews originate from?

Over the course of the centuries, religiously inspired myths that originated in the Middle Ages affixed themselves to more economically tinted stereotypes and prejudices about Jews. Right from the start, the theological outbursts directed at the Jews by the Protestant Reformer Martin Luther were laced with sharp condemnations of the Jewish moneylender – no doubt the classic antisemitic stereotype of all time. As with most stereotypes, this image contains a grain of truth. From the late Middle Ages until modern times, Jews were often the only people lending money in any given vicinity. Kings and the aristocracy frequently had Jewish financiers in their service. In Christian Poland – a country with a

A SOUTH AFRICAN CORPORATION.

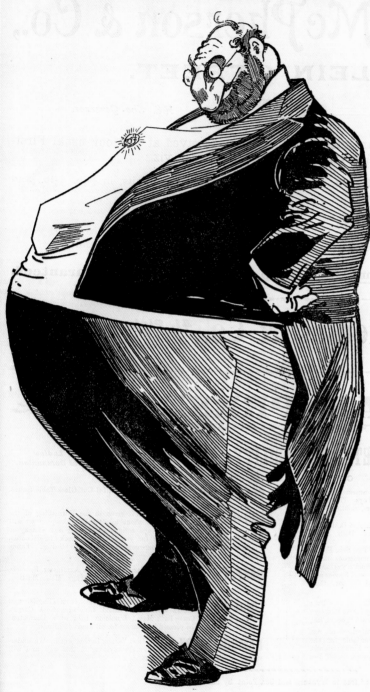

ITS LIMIT.

(WITH APOLOGIES TO "HOP.")

"I am of opinion that when the war . . . is over, and South Africa is . . . , there will be no limit to the size of these corporations.'—*John Morley.*

large Jewish community – the financial middlemen between farmers and noblemen were often Jews. They were employed to collect the rent from farmers who leased their land from the aristocracy. Moneylending was one of the few professions that Jews were allowed to practice and in a sense it contributed to the Jewish community being able to survive. For (exorbitant) fees, rich Jews could purchase the protection of secular rulers. However, they were never really sure of their position. Yet, not all Jews dealt in money. Most Jews in Europe were small farmers who lived in poverty. Trading and moneylending were only set aside for a small minority.

The personification of the Jewish moneylender is Shylock, the character created by the English playwright William Shakespeare in the year 1600. In the *Merchant of Venice*, Shylock lends a merchant named Antonio 3000 gold ducats. In turn, Antonio signs a letter of credit stating if he cannot repay the loan then Shylock may cut a pound of flesh from his body. Antonio loses the money he borrows and Shylock wants to collect on the debt. A trial ensues in which Shylock finally loses. He is forced to convert to Christianity or face death. Two of the most compelling antisemitic images of Shakespeare's time are united in the figure of Shylock: the Jewish moneylender and the Jew who is out for the blood of Christians. This combination of Jews and money also served as a strong source of stereotypes and prejudices later on in history. Several Socialist texts of the nineteenth and twentieth centuries blamed Jews for Capitalism and the monstrosity of abuses it created. The "rich Jew" was frequently the most prominent Jew and thus became a symbol for all Jews. Karl Marx, of Jewish ancestry himself, essentially considered Judaism and Capitalism one and the same. In his 1844 pamphlet *Zur Judenfrage* (The Jewish Question), he called Judaism the contemporary antisocial element: "What is the secular basis of Judaism? Practical need, self-interest. What is the worldly religion of the Jew? Huckstering. What is his worldly God? Money." However, in his booklet, Marx neglected to mention millions of nameless Jews of that period: poor peddlers, hawkers and factory workers.

Shakespeare

Shakespeare could not have had much first-hand experience with Jews. During his lifetime, hardly any Jews lived in England because all of them had already been expelled from England in the year 1290.

About the History of Antisemitism

FAGIN'S POLITICAL SCHOOL.

"Now, mark this; because these are things which you may not have heard in any speech which has been made in the city of Edinburgh. (*Laughter and cheers.*) I had—if it be not arrogant to use such a phrase—*to educate our party*. It is a large party, and requires its attention to be called to questions of this kind with some pressure. I had to prepare the mind of Parliament and the country on this question of Reform."—Mr. Disraeli's *Speech at the Edinburgh Banquet.*

Only a few descendants of Jews who had fled Spain and Portugal – Conversos (Jews who had converted to Christianity) – lived in the English capital at the end of the sixteenth century. It is not entirely clear if the *Merchant of Venice* was based on an Italian novella of the fourteenth century or if Shakespeare was inspired by the play the *Jew of Malta* by Christopher Marlowe, which was successfully performed in London in 1589. The first sentence that Shylock utters in the *Merchant of Venice* consists of only a few words: "Three thousand ducats; well." According to the American Jewish writer Philip Roth, these few small words have contributed to the stigmatization of Jews for centuries, and even today they continue to exert some degree of influence.

Fagin

In his book *Oliver Twist*, the English writer Charles Dickens rendered a grotesque caricature in the figure of the Jewish moneylender Fagin. Written between 1837 and 1839, this book is a fervent protest against the Poor Law adopted by the English Parliament in 1834. The book is also a parable: a battle between good and evil – symbolized by the youngster Oliver Twist and the Jewish miser Fagin. Fagin is not just any ordinary scoundrel, but a traditional Jewish hawker of the Middle Ages. Dickens portrays him in an extremely negative light, complete with hooked nose and beady eyes. Later in his career, Dickens regretted this antisemitic caricature. He scrapped many passages about Fagin being Jewish in a revised version of *Oliver Twist*, and a sympathetic Jew is portrayed as a character in one of his last novels.

17 Where does the concept of the worldwide Jewish conspiracy come from?

The legend that "the Jews" are out to dominate the world played an important role in the National Socialist propaganda of Germany in the first half of the twentieth century. Even though the myth of a worldwide Jewish conspiracy has its roots in the Middle Ages (see question 15), it was revitalized at the beginning of the twentieth century in Russia with the release of the book: *The Protocols of the Elders of Zion.* No other antisemitic text has been so widely

distributed or has had such a vitriolic effect. The famous American auto manufacturer Henry Ford, a rabid antisemite, had the *Protocols* translated into English in the 1920s and was responsible for the book being widely distributed in the United States. The Catholic Church has distributed this text in scores of European countries. Today, large numbers of copies of the *Protocols* are printed in the Arab world. In 2002, Egyptian television launched a major soap-opera series based on the *Protocols.* This television series, entitled *Horseman Without a Horse,* has been broadcast in many Arab countries. The *Protocols* are also distributed on the Internet via several right-wing extremist websites.

Based essentially on a hodge-podge of literary material from the second half of the nineteenth century, the *Protocols* "provide an account" of twenty-four secret gatherings of the so-called Elders of Zion, an anonymous group of rich and power-hungry Jews. These men gather to discuss the question of how they can destroy the Christian community and establish a Jewish world order. In their struggle against Church and State, the Elders of Zion make use of the lodges of Freemasons. The *Protocols* were first published in a newspaper in St. Petersburg in 1903 and other releases quickly followed – versions often differing extensively from each other. Contrary to what is often believed, the *Protocols* had little influence in Russia before the Revolution. Yet, afterwards opponents of Communism made quick use of them in their struggle against "Jewish Bolshevism". Before World War II, the Catholic Church in various European countries used the *Protocols* to depict the Jews as adversaries of Christianity. The *Protocols* themselves are an outstanding example of just how effective a conspiracy theory can be!

Anonymous
Who was responsible for writing the first *Protocols* has never been ascertained; the writer(s) remain(s) anonymous. According to one hypothesis, the text was written in Paris by one or more members of the *Okhrana* – the Czarist secret police that operated in France from around 1885 until the Russian Revolution in 1917. Another hypothesis suggests that the journalist who first published the *Protocols* in St. Petersburg was also the author (or one of the authors). Allegedly, the text was Frenchified at a later date. No matter where or how this work originated, there can be absolutely no doubt as to the fictitious nature of the *Protocols*.

Henry Ford

In the 1920s, the famous American car manufacturer Henry Ford financed the publication of an English-language version of the *Protocols of the Elders of Zion.* This translation was serialized for many years in the *Dearborn Independent,* a weekly newspaper personally backed by him and distributed among Ford factory workers free of charge. Henry Ford was one of the richest and most influential American industrialists of his time. In 1927, however, he apologized to the Jewish community in America for this antisemitic campaign, an apology he publicly repeated in 1942. Since that time, to rid themselves of the stigma of antisemitism, the Ford family and their factories have financially supported all kinds of projects to help the Jewish community in America.

The American auto manufacturer Henry Ford was a rabid antisemite and personally financed the publication of an English translation of the *Protocols of the Elders of Zion.*

Alexandria

In 2003, a copy of the *Protocols of the Elders of Zion* was displayed next to a copy of the Torah at an exhibition mounted in the Great Library of Alexandria. This library, built to replace the famous ancient library that was unfortunately destroyed by fire, had opened a year earlier with the mandate to function as a center for dialogue and culture. After a wave of protests in the Israeli and Egyptian press, the copy of the *Protocols* was removed from the exhibition.

18 What is true about the powerful Jewish lobby in the United States?

One of the classic modern-day myths is that "the Jews are running the show" in the United States of America. The huge influence exerted by a Jewish lobby is accordingly often mentioned in the same breath. For some people, the power exerted by this lobby is proof that Israel – if only in secret – is also pulling the strings in America. Different than in the Netherlands, political lobbying is institutionalized in the United States. Organized groups who want promote certain affairs and points-of-view to the Washington D.C. politicians – who eventually get to vote on these issues – can be officially registered in America. This gives them access to Capitol Hill – the legislative branch of the American government – and on occasion even to the White House, which is the executive

About the History of Antisemitism

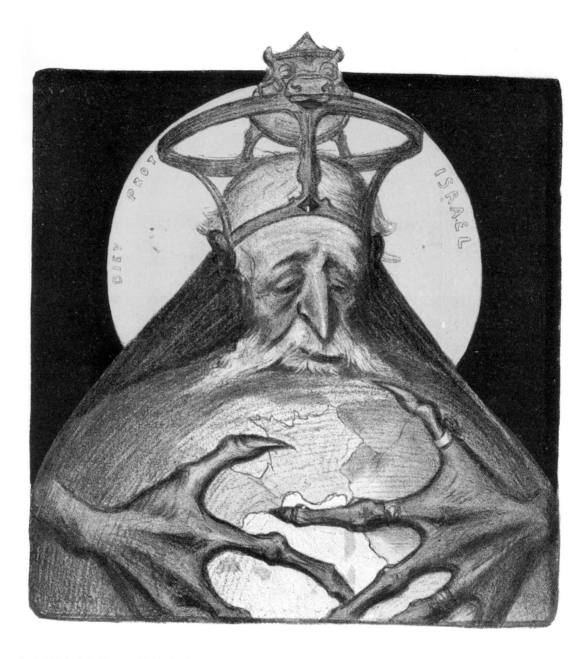

The Jewish banker Rothschild as a symbol of the Jewish aspiration to dominate the
world. French caricature, 1898.

Al-Watan (Kuwait), February 17, 2003.

Al-Ahram (Egypt), December 26, 2002.

Israel has the ear of the United Nations, while the Palestinians are held at arms distance. *Al-Hayat Al-Jadida* (Palestinian Authority), November 16, 2002.

An American bridegroom to his Jewish bride: "Okay, you have the final word, but I am the man of the house!" *Al-Ittihad* (Israel) August 1, 2002.

branch of power. It is actually more accurate to speak of a pro-Israel lobby instead of a Jewish lobby. The pro-Israel lobby in the Untied States is made up of more than just Jewish organizations. By far, the largest pro-Israel lobby in the Untied States is the American Israeli Public Affairs Committee (AIPAC). With its staff of around a hundred people and access to a yearly budget of thirteen million dollars, the AIPAC serves as an umbrella organization for practically all American-Jewish institutions. The Jewish community in America is incredibly diverse and often divided on many of the issues – that is except one: practically everybody supports the existence and continued survival of the State of Israel. According to the American magazine *Forbes*, AIPAC is the third most influential lobby operating in Washington D.C. The gun lobby, united under the National Rifle Association (NRA) and the Senior lobby known as the American Association of Retired People (AARP) rank as numbers one and two. Contrary to what many people think, politicians and political candidates are not supported or financed by AIPAC. In addition to the pro-Israel lobby in Washington, there is also a pro-Arab lobby that has been active longer but is much smaller. The influence that lobbying exerts on American Middle -Eastern policy is generally overestimated. Articles appearing in newspapers or on the Internet related to this topic claim that the pro-Israel lobby has a huge influence, and actually dictates American foreign policy. However, these articles are usually not supported by the facts. An extensive survey of more than 780 actual cases of policymaking and points-of-view related to the Middle East indicated that the pro-Israel lobby succeeded in convincing the American Congress in 60 percent of cases. In situations in which the points-of-view of AIPAC and the American president clashed, the American Congress sided with AIPAC in only 27 percent of all cases. On the whole, the primary reason the pro-Israel lobby in the United States is so successful is because members of both the Republican and Democratic parties, and politicians as well as the voters all back the most important objective of AIPAC: supporting the State of Israel.

19 Are Wall Street and Hollywood controlled by Jews?

"What Every Congressman Should Know": the Jews control America. An antisemitic pamphlet that was distributed in the Untied States in 1939.

The Polish-Jewish immigrants Samuel Goldwyn (1882-1974), Jack Warner (1892-1978) and Louis B. Mayer (1885-1957) were influential in establishment of the great Hollywood film studios. Goldwyn, born as Schmuel Gelb-fisz, and Mayer, born as Lazar Mayer, worked their way up in the movie business and headed MGM Studios. Warner, born as Jack Leonard Eichelbaum, ran Warner Brothers with his brother Harry.

The idea that Jews control Wall Street and Hollywood is a modern-day rendition of the classic antisemitic myth that Jews are out for power and world domination. This story not only turns up in the United States, but all over the world. According to random opinion polls that have been conducted, at least a third of the American population believes that Jews have too much power on Wall Street. Stories about the Jewish influence exerted on the American media and the financial world – similar to other conspiracy theories – are contemporary antisemitic legends that are difficult to refute with facts and figures There are no exact records kept of how many Jews work in Hollywood or on Wall Street. Yet, even if there were, people who believe this myth would not be convinced by the statistics. Nobody can deny that Polish-Jewish immigrants such as Samuel Goldwyn, Jack and Harry Warner, and Louis B. Mayer were influential in the establishment of the great Hollywood film studios. Yet, what few people know is that Hollywood also has its own history of antisemitism. At the beginning of the twentieth century, large production companies such as Universal and Keystone made so-called Jew movies: films that portrayed Jews as criminals who were stingy and sly. These "Jew movies" were quite popular and an average of two per week were produced. It was only when Universal Studios finally stopped producing these sorts of films that other companies followed suit. Nevertheless, in his public antisemitic campaigns of the 1920s, Henry Ford doggedly hammered home the idea that: "The motion picture influence of the United States and Canada is exclusively under the control, moral and financial, of the Jewish manipulators of the public mind." Today, these sorts of haunting images, for example on the Internet, are still widely

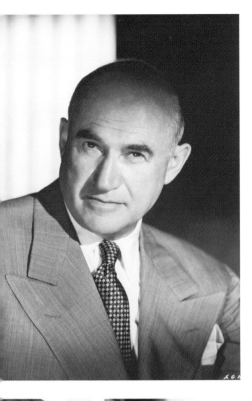

Once every ten years, the residents of the German town of Oberammergau (in the Bavarian Alps) mount a huge production of the Passion Play. The version that was performed in the year 2000, in which more than two thousand extras participated, was stripped of the many anti-Jewish passages previously so characteristic of this work. The past performance of Passion Plays has often stirred-up anti-Jewish feelings.

The film *The Passion of The Christ*, made by actor and director Mel Gibson, is a screen adaptation of the suffering and death of Christ. The film received much criticism because of its profuse use of violence and its anti-Jewish leanings.

spread. Not only are these stories completely unfounded, most of the important film studios in Hollywood are now in the hands of foreign investors and banks. Moreover, American Jews active in the film industry today work there as individuals, not as representatives of their religious or ethnic group and certainly not with the intention to conspire. Obviously, this same reasoning applies to the myth about the Jewish influence on Wall Street. Similar to Europe, a few Jewish bankers in the Untied States rose to prominent positions in the last hundred to hundred-fifty years. Nevertheless, the fact that individual Jews have been successful in the world of banking and business in America does not immediately imply anything about the "Jewish influence" on Wall Street. Insofar as Jews are active in society or in the business world, they do this as individuals, not as Jews representing their ethnic or religious group. This prejudice is not about linking the words Jew and Wall Street to each other, or even the words Jew and Hollywood. It is instead about how notions such as influence, control, and power are combined with the word Jew.

Mel Gibson

The feature-film *The Passion of the Christ* by Mel Gibson, which first appeared in movie theaters in 2004, tells the story of the Passion, an account of the suffering and death of Jesus Christ on the Cross. In earlier times in Europe, the depiction of the Passion story – for example presented in public (Passion Play) – was often just enough provocation needed to stir up anti-Jewish feelings. "After all, hadn't the Jews killed Jesus?" Prior to its release, Mel Gibson's rather bloody and violent film had already received a critical reception from Jewish organizations in America, fearful that the film would stir up Jew-hatred. This very same pre-publicity partly contributed to the film becoming a box-office success in American and Europe. Moreover, the film also attracted many viewers in the Middle East. Despite the fact that according to the Koran, Jesus Christ – an important prophet for Muslims – was not crucified and did not die but was taken up to heaven by Allah. The reaction to this film in the Muslim world was equally remarkable, given that the depiction of prophets and persons from the Koran is not only very unusual, but essentially forbidden.

20 Are all Jews rich?

The remark one often hears about all Jews being rich is one of the oldest and most persistent prejudices. A level-headed look at socio-economic figures is enough to contradict this bias. One out of five families in present-day Israel live under the poverty level. According to figures of the National Insurance Institute – the official governmental body in Israel that oversees income benefits (Welfare) for the social security system – as many as one in three children in Israel live in poverty. Research in the United States indicates that 11 to 12 percent of American Jews live under the poverty level, a figure in keeping with the national average. Almost 20 percent of American Jews live in a family that has less than 25,000 dollars a year available for spending. This category in the United States borders on low income or "almost poor". The socio -economic position of the average Jew is roughly comparable to the average American. There are no figures available about the Jews living in the Netherlands, though history illustrates that many European Jews were poor and frequently very poor. Of course, there have always been rich Jews too. They were regularly of vital importance to the continued existence of the Jewish community. In numerous European countries, Jews were assessed for taxes as one economic unit. The money generated by rich Jews played a central role in the ability of Jewish communities to survive. These communities had to care for their own poor and were

About the History of Antisemitism

Before World War II, a large part
of the working class Jews of
Amsterdam lived crammed into
the one-room apartments of
narrow streets and alleyways.

essentially self-supporting. In Dutch history, the small Sephardic community was on the average more well to do than the much larger Ashkenazi community. A hundred years ago, most families in Amsterdam's Jewish neighborhood lived in dire poverty. The majority of Jews living in Russia, Poland, and the Austro-Hungarian Empire – a hundred years ago the three countries with by far the largest Jewish populations – were terribly poor as well. Violent pogroms in Russia partially contributed to these Jews fleeing, but the huge Jewish immigration from Poland and the Austro-Hungarian Empire to the United States around the year 1900, was almost exclusively motivated by economic factors. In that same period, the Jews who lived in the countries surrounding the Mediterranean were probably the worst off economically. Jewish communities in the western European countries, with France at the lead, conducted campaigns to raise money to help Jews living in North Africa. Down through the centuries, the singling out of prominent Jewish bankers and business people has supported the prejudice that all Jews are rich. Prejudice is given credence when examples are provided as confirmation. What tends to apply, whether one looks at the past or the present, is that affluence is usually more visible than poverty. Well-to-do individuals often actively participate in all aspects of a society and are inclined to appear in the foreground. They are therefore more noticeable. Poor people are often ashamed of their poverty and prefer to conceal it by fading into the background.

Many Jews in Eastern Europe lived below poverty level before World War II. This 1923 photo was taken in Vilna, Lithuania – at that moment part of the Soviet Union – and shows two Jewish beggars on the steps of the old synagogue.

Fifty Ques-tions on Antisem-itism

21 thru 29
About Jews, Christians, Muslims

21 Have Jews and Christians always been each other's enemies?

The Church – symbolized here by the standing Ecclesia – is portrayed victorious over Judaism, the Synagogue lying at her feet. The Cross – the symbol of Christ – is firmly held to the throat of the blindfolded Synagogue. Jews were frequently depicted in the Middle Ages wearing blindfolds. They were blind or sightless because they did not recognize Jesus Christ as the Messiah. This twelfth century prayer book illustration is from the North of France.

The pontificate of Pope Pius IX lasted 32 years; he was the longest reigning pope in history. Pio Nono, as he was also called, was furthermore one of the most anti-Jewish popes of all time. In 1870, he once referred to Jews as dogs: "There are too many of them and we hear them whimpering in the streets."

Over the last two thousand years, Christians and Jews have basically been each other's religious rivals. Christianity often perceived (and still perceives) itself as the continuation or the replacement of Judaism. Jews, in turn, have never accepted the main religious tenet of the Christian Church – that Jesus Christ is the Son of God and the Messiah (the "anointed one"). To refute each other's theologies, Christians and Jews have found themselves engaged in controversial discussions and disputes. Many Christians saw Jews as "God-killers" (see question 25) or to a lesser extreme, as heretics who still needed to be converted either by the power of persuasion or with coercion and brutality. European history has frequently exhibited a lack of religious tolerance. The Crusades and the Inquisition are cruel and bloody examples of this. However, there were extended periods in which Jews and Christians live alongside each other in harmony. If the entire Jewish history of Europe had only been about twenty centuries of persecution, then long ago there would already been no Jews left in Europe. Spain during the Middle Ages – the European country with the largest Jewish population at that time – had great respect for religious tolerance. The legendary Caliphate of Cordoba in the tenth century – when a large part of Spain fell under Muslim rule – was tolerant of both Christians and Jews. Even when Christian monarchs "reconquered" a major portion of Spain from Muslim rulers in the thirteenth and fourteenth centuries, Jews, Christians and Muslims continued to peacefully lived among each other for hundreds of years. These were mostly prosperous times for all three communities and culture flourished.

According to the historian Norman Roth, Spain was the only truly pluralistic society of the Middle Ages (today we would say multi-ethnic). This finally all went wrong in the late Middle Ages during the fifteenth century. In 1492, the last Muslim kingdom and the Jews were driven from Spain. The Catholic Church has zealously condemned the "unbelieving" Jews with its words and decrees for centuries. Anti-Judaism was an abiding aspect of Catholicism up until the twentieth century. One could easily compile a long list of anti-Jewish statements and edicts issued by the Papal authority. In the Papal State – disbanded with the Unification of Italy in 1870 – the Jews suffered under discriminatory restrictions longer than anywhere else in Europe. The ghetto of Rome was the last "real" Jewish ghetto. The Church finally took steps in the 1960s – following the Second Vatican Council – to sort out its anti-Jewish past. The current Pope John Paul II is the first pope in history to have visited a synagogue and publicly admitted culpability in the name of the Church.

Crusades

The Crusades in the twelfth and thirteenth centuries benefited from the active support of the Catholic Church. Farmers, knights, adventurers, and at times even children departed from their homes in Europe – usually on foot and spurred on by the Cross – to recapture the Holy Land of Palestine from the Muslims. The history of the Crusades is a long line of bloody incidents that have influenced, up until the present day, the image that Christians and Muslims have of each other. Generally less well known is that the Jews were often the first victims of the Crusades. In cities such as Trier, Mainz, Worms and Cologne, the Christian Crusaders presented Jews with "a choice" to convert or face death. A large amount of Jews died: probably a third of all the Jews who lived in Europe north of the Alps were murdered by these crusading knights. While Church Officials of the time often condemned the violence of the Crusaders against the Jews, the violence perpetrated against Muslims and heretics was simply condoned.

The Inquisition

The Holy Office of the Catholic Church – also known as the Inquisition – existed from the twelfth to the nineteenth century. The Inquisition was established to return heretics to the fold. This was accomplished in many countries by the use of force. The Inquisition in Spain at the end of the fifteenth and in the first half of the sixteenth century was especially notorious. Contrary to what many people think, this Inquisition was less directed at Jews than fallen and heretical Christians. Conversos, a large group of former Jews who had converted en masse to Christianity a century earlier were also among the many victims of the Inquisition. During an *auto-da-fe* (test of faith), a sort of mix between a religious gathering and a public trial, Conversos were called upon to account for themselves and then burned at the stake as heretics (a punishment also reserved for witches).

Anti-Jewish Popes

Very few popes in history have chosen to defend the Jews. However, one could name many who issued anti-Jewish edicts and laws or who publicly made anti-Jewish statements. Until well into the nineteenth century, the Pope in Rome was also the secular leader of what was then called the Papal State. Jews in the Papal State had to wear a yellow emblem clearly displayed on their clothing and were punished for not doing so also well into the nineteenth century. The race laws of the Italian Fascists in the 1930s and the Nuremberg Race Laws of the Nazis, which robbed the Jews in Italy and Germany of their rights as citizens, were partly modeled on discriminatory measures toward Jews that the Catholic Church had been using for centuries.

22 Have Jews and Muslims always been each other's enemies?

Similar to Christianity, Islam has much religious ground in common with Judaism. Muslims believe in one God, as do Jews and Christians. However, a number of important differences exist between Islam and Christianity in their relationship to Judaism. The central figure of Christianity – Jesus of Nazareth, who Christians consider the Son of God – was a Jew. In contrast, the founder of Islam – the prophet Mohammed – was not a Jew but an Arab. Mohammed was also never considered a Messiah, but always a prophet – "the" Prophet to be more precise. In addition, for Muslims the Koran is a new revelation and not the fulfillment of earlier Jewish prophecies as the New Testament is for Christians. Christianity was a Jewish sect in the beginning and it later attracted non-Jews who choose to follow this new religious belief. While the Christianization of heathens in Europe took many centuries, in contrast, Muslim warriors conquered a large part of the world in a relatively short amount of time. Islam quickly spread from Central Asia to Southern Spain and not only due to the use of force. Around the year 900, after Islam had been introduced all over this huge region, approximately 1 percent of the population was made up of Jews. Christians and Jews have always

A Jewish woman in Morocco, before World War II.

A Jewish wedding in Morocco before World War II. At that time, part of the country was a French protectorate. However, the Jews in Morocco usually had fewer problems with antisemitism than Jews living in France.

been seen in the Muslim world as "People of the Book", respectively the New Testament (Christian Bible) and the Tanach (Hebrew or Jewish Bible). In the *dar al-Islam* – the world of Islam – they always enjoyed more protection than heathens. Nonetheless, for centuries, they were subject to the rules of the Dhimma Statutes: in exchange for payment of protection money and extra taxes, they were granted the status of second-class citizens. Bearing in mind a few exceptions, one can safely say that Jews and Muslims have not always been each other's enemies. For fourteen centuries, Jewish minorities lived in peace in many countries and under many regimes in the Muslim world. Yet, comparable to the history of Christian Europe, besides its peaceful periods and tolerant regimes, Islam has also experienced warlike regimes and intolerant periods. Under the rule of many Ottoman Sultans, for example, the religious climate was relatively tolerant. While in Iran, during the time of the Safawids – a mighty Shiite dynasty that ruled a large part of the Middle East from 1501 to 1722 – the climate toward religious minorities was extremely intolerant. At that time, not only Jews but also Christians and followers of other religious prophets, such as Zarathustra, were regularly harassed, persecuted and forced to convert.

Dhimmis

In the *dar al-Islam*, Jews and Christians alike were called dhimmis and forced to live by different rules than Muslims. According to oral tradition, the Dhimma Statutes dated back to the time of the first Caliph, Omar 1 (634-644 C.E.). However, these statutes, known as the "Pact of Omar", were only set-down on parchment a hundred years later. The pact primarily demanded that Christians and Jews show respect for Islam and Muslims. Dhimmis were not allowed to carry weapons, ride horses, and were required to wear special clothing or certain identifying emblems on their garments to easily distinguish from Muslims. Countless other humiliating rules were also forced upon them. They had to pay higher taxes and sometimes hand over these taxes to the local authorities in public. Though the Dhimma Statutes were put into effect everywhere in the Muslim world, they were only enforced to varying degrees.

In early days in the world of Islam, Jews could be recognized by emblems displayed on their clothing (a yellow mark for example). The color white was reserved for Muslims; Jews generally had to wear black. This photograph of a Jewish man was taken in Morocco before World War II.

The Jewish Wife of Mohammed

Tales about the life of the prophet Mohammed and his family play an important role in Islamic tradition. Practically everything we know about him is based on oral tradition. Mohammed was born around the year 570 in Mecca to the clan of Hashim and his death in 632 C.E. marked the beginning of the Islamic calendar. In Mohammed's time, a number of Jewish clans also lived in Mecca and Medina. After his struggle with and victory over these Jewish clans (see question 27), he married a Jewish woman who had been taken as a prisoner. Her name was Safiya and she became one of his many wives. Even though the Koran states that a man may only have four wives (Surah 33:51), the Prophet was exempted from this rule.

23 Did Jews live better in the past under Islam than under Christianity?

It is difficult, if not impossible to compare fourteen centuries of Islam to twenty centuries of Christianity. Discrimination against Jews occurred in the Islamic world on a regular basis but they were rarely persecuted. Even though the history of Christian Europe was rather different, some striking similarities can be noted. Jews were often forced to wear distinctive clothing or emblems. It is hard to retrace where this might have begun, but wearing a stigmatizing yellow emblem probably originated in the Islamic world. As early as the beginning of the ninth century, Caliph Haroen al-Rasjid ordered the Jews to wear a piece of yellow cloth. In many European countries starting in the thirteenth century, Jews were first required to wear a yellow mark on their clothing and later a yellow circle resembling a ring. The yellow cloth patch – in the shaped of a Jewish Star of David – that the National Socialists (Nazis) decreed Jews must wear in the 1940s, carried on an age-old tradition. In Christian Europe, much energy was devoted to coercing Jews to repudiate their religious beliefs. For centuries, Christians zealously tried to convert Jews; this occurred much less under Islam (see question 28). During these times, numerous Christian theologians, philosophers and Church Officials were guilty of exaggerating antisemitic legends and stereotypes. In past centuries, Muslim scholars and Islamic writers have been far less guilty of this. Early Muslim literature contains no "Jewish monsters" such as Shylock in Shakespeare's the *Merchant of Venice* or Fagin in Charles Dickens' *Oliver Twist*. Antisemitic stereotypes first appeared in the Muslim world in the

The Catholic Rulers responsible for creating the Spanish State – King Ferdinand of Aragon and Queen Isabella of Castile – forced the Jews to leave the country in 1492. A dynamic and rich Jewish life that had flourished for fifteen centuries came to an end on most of the Iberian Peninsula. This painting from Emilio Sala Francés, entitled *Expulsión de los judíos* (Expulsion of the Jews) dates from 1889 and is hanging in the Prado Museum in Madrid.

About Jews, Christians, Muslims

nineteenth century when large parts of the Arab world were conquered by European colonial powers. It is striking that almost all the antisemitic myths that proliferate the Arab world today were fashioned in the Christian or Western world.

Convivencia

Medieval Spain – from the time of the Muslim conquests in the year 711 until the expulsion of the Jews in 1492 – had the largest Jewish community in Europe for centuries. This era, particularly in the Muslim part of Spain called al-Andalus, was a golden age in many respects. It was a time when Jewish, Christian, and Islamic arts and sciences flourished: the most beautiful Moorish palaces were built, calligraphers and illustrators created beautiful Torah scrolls, Bibles, and Korans, and Jewish linguists translated Latin texts into Arabic and Arabic texts into Latin. Jews played an important role at the court of Abd al-Rahman III (912-961) who ruled the Caliphate of Cordoba for fifty years. Spanish historians have given this period an appropriate name: *Convivencia*, which also translates as "living together in good company".

The famous Jewish philosopher Rabbi Mozes ben Maimon (1135-1204), better known as Maimonides, lived and worked in Cordoba (at that time the capital of Al-Andalus). When the Muslim Fundamentalist Almohads of North Africa conquered the city, he fled the country. Maimonides wrote in Arabic and toward the end of his life also served as the personal physician to the sultan of Egypt.

24 Is the New Testament antisemitic?

The almost two thousand year old religious struggle between Jews and Christians has revolved around the degree of truthfulness of the Scriptures known as the New Testament (Christian Bible). Christians believe that Jesus Christ is the Son of God and the Messiah. While Muslims see Jesus only as a prophet and Judaism acknowledges him as a teacher – a "rabbi". To an impartial reader, the Scriptures of Jesus – as set down in the four Gospels – are at certain moments extremely critical if not entirely negative towards Jews and Judaism. In many chapters, such as Matthew 23, Jewish teachers of the law are sharply condemned. They are reproached for being blind and hypocritical as well as unyielding regarding interpretation and enforcement of the laws and commandments. John 19 portrays the Jews calling for the Crucifixion of Jesus (see question 25). These and other anti-Jewish passages have not only been used in past disputations with the Jewish "unbeliever" (in Christ), but they have also been used against Jews in ways that led to persecution and banishment. Not only is there discussion among theologians and Church historians as to whether the New Testament has encouraged antisemitism, there is also the question of whether the New Testament is inherently antisemitic. This question cannot be answered with a simple yes or no. What we actually know about the historic figure of Jesus and the origins and time frame of the writing of the four Gospels is extremely limited and unreliable, so this discussion will certainly continue. Was Jesus, as some Jewish theologians claim, simply a Jewish teacher who lived according to the Torah and did not reject his own people and faith? The idea of a Messiah who first has to suffer and die – and who leaves the world behind unchanged – completely contradicts the Messianic vision as described in Judaism. Have Church Fathers and Christian theologians stripped Jesus of too

Paul, the "Apostle of the Heretics", criticized the "unbelieving" Jews in his letters. He is shown here in a disputation with the Jews: the New Testament versus the Old Testament. The Jews in this panel from the twelfth century are depicted wearing the Jew hat.

much of his Jewishness? These kinds of questions – intriguing for theologians and other religious enthusiasts – are difficult to answer.

Paul

The Apostle Paul, whose letters are included in the New Testament, was the first missionary and the actual founder of what later became the Christian Church. Many Christians refer to Paul as the "Apostle of the Heretics", the man who used words and deeds to convince others that Jesus Christ was the Messiah, not only of the Jewish people but of the entire world. Thanks to Paul, an early Jewish sect evolved into a Church for non-Jews and grew into the worldwide religion of Christianity in the centuries that followed. A number of Jewish historians, however, believe that Paul's ideas in particular contributed to the later anti-Jewish sentiments of the Christian Church. In several passages in his letters, Paul is rather negative about the "unbelieving" Jews. His letters were regularly used in later centuries to widen the religious gap between Jews and Christians.

25 Why have so many Christians seen the Jews as the murderers of Christ?

The crucifixion of Christ, with the Christians lit brightly (left) and the Jews blindfolded (right) beneath the Cross. Germany, fifteenth century.

Throughout history, the most significant accusation that Christians have leveled against Jews is that they murdered Jesus Christ. The animosity of Christians toward Jews and Judaism has been fueled by this idea for centuries. The Gospel of John from the New Testament (Christian Bible) was used to support the belief that the Jews were the "murderers of God". In John 19:15 the Jews call for the Crucifixion of Jesus: "Take him away! Take him away! Crucify him!" Also, the Gospel of Matthew 27:25, when the Jews cry out: "Let his blood be on us and on our children!" is often quoted for this same purpose. The idea of the Jew as "Christ-killer" strongly contributed to the persecution of Jews in Europe. Apart from the theologically fascinating question of whether it is even possible to kill the Son of God, or any god

Augustine (354-430), Bishop of Hippo, saw the Diaspora of the Jewish people as their punishment for the crucifixion of Jesus. This fresco of him, painted by Sandro Botticelli, is located in the Eglise Ognissanti (Florence), the church where the famous painter is also buried. The fresco dates from 1480.

The Crucifixion of Christ, with Ecclesia symbolizing the Church (left) and a blindfolded Jew (right). Ecclesia is holding the staff with the pennant; the Jew's staff is broken. From the Cologne School of painting, fifteenth century.

for that matter, a few historical remarks should be taken into account regarding this accusation of "God's murder". The four Gospels of the New Testament state that Jesus died on a cross; in those times, a typically Roman way of putting people to death. According to Jewish law of that era, stoning was the common death penalty. Besides, Jesus was condemned by the Procurator of Judea Pontius Pilate – the Roman authority at that time – and even according to the earliest Christian Creed: "[Jesus] was crucified also for us under Pontius Pilate; He suffered and was buried…" He did not suffer under the Pharisees, the Jewish sect portrayed in the Gospel of Matthew as the archenemies of Jesus and his followers. He also did not suffer at the hand of the Jewish High Priest Caiaphas. Christianity's claim, that the Jews, not the Romans, sentenced and executed Jesus mainly evolved out of the latter-day religious rivalry between Jews and Christians. In the early centuries of its existence, Christianity developed from a small Jewish sect into a Church for non-Jews. The accusation of "God's murder" played a central role in that development. Apart from this, the idea of a Messiah that first has to suffer and die is unacceptable from a Jewish perspective. The relentless accusation of Christ's murder – both directly and indirectly – led to much bloodshed, especially during the Crusades of the Middle Ages. This myth was a central doctrine of the Catholic Church until the twentieth century. Only following the Second Vatican Council (1962-1965), did the standpoint of the Catholic Church toward Jews change. Yet, the story of the Jew as "Christ-killer" has never been truly put to rest and it still regularly resurfaces. For example, in a letter written in 2001 about the present conflict between Israel and the Palestinians, the Greek Orthodox Patriarch in Jerusalem expressed his support for Yasser Arafat's struggle against Israel and referred to the Israelis as: "… the descendants of the crucifiers of our Lord, actual crucifiers of your people…."

Augustine of Hippo

One of the most influential Christian theologians and philosophers in European history was Aurelius Augustine (354-430), Bishop of the North African coastal town of Hippo (in present-day Tunisia). At the time of Augustine, many Jews lived in North Africa. In his *Tractate Against the Jews*, Augustine described the Diaspora of the Jewish people as their punishment for the Crucifixion of Jesus.

He believed that the Jewish people were robbed of God's mercy and thus – as Cain had been – cursed. However, he disapproved of the persecution of Jews, using the highly original argument that the ongoing existence of the Jewish people was a testimony to the truth of the Old Testament and therefore an assertion of the truth of the Church. As far as Augustine was concerned, Jews did not have to abandon their religion, customs and traditions in order for this evidence to prevail.

Nostra Aetate
"True, the Jewish authorities and those who followed their lead pressed for the death of Christ (John 19:6); still, what happened in his passion cannot be blamed upon all the Jews then living, without distinction, nor upon the Jews of today. Although the Church is the new people of God, the Jews should not be presented as rejected or accursed by God, as if this followed from the Holy Scriptures." This statement is excerpted from Nostra Aetate, a 1965 decree (proclamation) issued by the Vatican about the position of the Catholic Church concerning non-Christian religions. Subsequent to the Second Vatican Council and with this decree, Pope Paul VI officially retracted the accusation of many of his predecessors: that the Jews were collectively responsible for the death of Christ.

26 Have Catholics always been more anti-Jewish than Protestants?

The Christian Church of Northern, Western, and Middle Europe was shattered in the sixteenth century. This break within the Church, which came to be known as the Reformation, was the beginning of different Protestant religious denominations. Many Protestants, starting with the German Church reformer Martin Luther, fervently opposed Judaism. Once it had become evident that the Jews of Europe would not join him in his struggle against the Catholic Church, he published a harsh anti-Jewish pamphlet entitled: *Von den Juden und ihren Lügen* (On Jews and Their Lies). Other prominent Church Reformers (such as Calvin and Zwingli) also did not deviate from the Catholic Church's official theology toward the Jews. The scattering of the Jewish people was seen for the most part as a divine punishment they had to endure (Diaspora) and Jews were there to be converted to the one true faith. The Jews who lived in places where the King and the population had converted to Protestantism were discriminated against and often persecuted, just as they had been in Catholic Europe. In contrast to Luther, John Calvin's texts were less bitter toward the Jews. This undoubtedly contributed to Calvinistic Holland being a relatively safe place for Jews to live from the seventeenth century and onward. Protestant denominations – ranging from Lutheran to Baptist and Dutch Reformed to Anglican – had comparatively less power than the Catholic Church. The Pope in Rome had his own state and his own armies for centuries. The Vatican exerted an influence on the policies of countries, far removed from Italy, if the majority of that country's population was Catholic. In contrast, an early tradition of separation of Church and State developed in the Protestant countries of Europe. While

IOHANNES CALVINVS
NATVS 1508.
OBYT 1564.

the Vatican displayed a harsh steadfast tradition of anti-Judaism throughout the centuries, the anti-Jewish stance of many Protestant denominations showed more diversity.

17. Titelblatt von Martin Luthers Schrift wider

Von den Juden und ihren Lügen (On Jews and Their Lies), a harsh anti-Jewish pamphlet dating from 1543 by the German Church Reformer Martin Luther.

Luther and Hitler

In his book *Mein Kampf* (My Struggle), Adolf Hitler praised the defamatory anti-Jewish texts of Martin Luther, who he greatly admired: "Luther was a great man, a giant. With one blast of the clarion, he proclaimed a new age…he saw the Jews the way we finally begin to see them now." In 1938, the Nazis dedicated *Kristallnacht* (The Night of Broken Glass) – when synagogues in Germany were vandalized and set aflame – to Luther. Though many historians see parallels between the writings of Luther and the antisemitic ideas of Hitler, it is too simplistic to draw a straight-line connecting the two. There are also huge disparities: the Lutheran Church never embraced the strong anti-Jewish attitude of its founder. Scandinavian countries such as Denmark, Norway, and Sweden for example, though predominantly Lutheran, did not develop antisemitic traditions.

27 What does the Koran say about Jews?

Jews as well as Christians have a unique status in Islam. Muslims believe that God passed on his will to the prophets Abraham (Ibrahim), Moses (Moesa) and Jesus (Isa). Mary, the mother of Jesus, appears in the Koran more than in the New Testament. There are also many references to the Torah and the Jewish prophets in the Koran. Jews are the descendants of Abraham and Sarah, while Muslims see themselves as descendants of Abraham and Hagar – the handmaid of Abraham's wife. The Koran says that Abraham (Ibrahim) was not a Jew but a Muslim (Surah 3:67-68). According to Islamic tradition, Ibrahim built the *Kaäba* – the sanctuary of Mecca – together with his son Ishmael. Muslims believe that God's original revelations to Moses and Jesus were passed down inaccurately; the revelations to the prophet Mohammed, as recorded in the Koran are the unique, eternal, true Word of God. Besides allusions to the Torah, the prophets, and the New Testament, the Koran also describes the clashes of Mohammed with the Jewish tribes of the Arabian Peninsula (present-day Saudi Arabia). Three Jewish tribes who did not want to convert to Islam lived there at the time of Mohammed. The Army of the Prophet expelled two of these tribes from Medina in 624 and 625. A few years later, the men of the third Jewish tribe were killed and their wives and children sold into slavery. Mohammed's conflict with the Jewish tribes of Medina is not one of the Koran's central themes; it is of minor importance. Yet, these Koran verses about the struggle of the Prophet against the Jews have been chanted repeatedly at anti-Israel demonstrations in the past few years.

The Jews of Medina

The prophet Mohammed displays an ambivalent attitude toward Jews. On the one hand, he respects the Jews as the recipients of the earliest divine revelations. Yet, on the other hand, he criticizes them for having distorted these very same revelations. Mohammed's conflict with the Jews of Medina leads to the destruction of the Jewish tribes. The myth of "God's murder", which has played such a major role in the attitude of Christians toward Jews, is not an aspect of Islam. Many Muslims believe that the conflict between Judaism and Islam was already resolved at the time of the Prophet and in favor of Islam.

Iniquity

Surah 4:160 from the Koran denounces the Jews: "Wherefore for the iniquity of those who are Jews did We disallow to them the good things which had been made lawful for them and for their hindering many (people) from Allah's way." In several other places in this Surah (chapter) – as well as in other verses of the Koran – the Jews of Medina unwilling to convert to Islam are not given another choice. Still, the attitude toward Jews at other moments in the Koran is quite positive. Surah 2:47 reads: "O children of Israel! call to mind My favor which I bestowed on you and that I made you excel the nations."

Oral Tradition

In all likelihood, Mohammed never read the Torah and only knew of the Holy Book of the Jews from oral tradition. As far as the Jews were concerned, his references to the Torah were often inaccurate. For example in Surah 28:38, the Prophet has the Egyptian Pharaoh (Book of Exodus) ask Haman (Book of Esther) to build the Tower of Babel (Book of Genesis). This is an example of the Prophet connecting stories and people from very different periods of Jewish history. The refusal of the Jews of Medina to accept Mohammed as a prophet could have been related to what they saw as his lack of knowledge of the Torah.

Mary, Mother of Jesus

Mary is the only woman in the Koran to whom an entire – and very poetic – Surah is devoted. According to Muslim tradition, Jesus and his mother were the only two human souls left untouched by the devil at birth. Specific aspects of the veneration of Mary in Islam most resemble the veneration of the Holy Virgin in Eastern Orthodox Christian tradition. For example, both accounts refer to the prophet Zacharias as Mary's guardian.

Mary, the mother of Jesus, is not only revered in Christianity. She is also the most admired woman of Islam. An entire Surah (chapter) of the Koran is dedicated to her. Depicting people from the Koran is forbidden in Muslim tradition, but is extremely commonplace in Christian tradition. This *Virgin and Child* was painted in the sixteenth century by Di Lorenzo and hangs in the National Gallery (London).

28 Why have many Jews converted to another religion in the past?

Down through the ages, millions of Jews have (been) converted to Christianity and Islam. This sometimes occurred using simple persuasion, at other times under duress, and occasionally brute force was involved. Jews often chose to convert for the obvious practical reasons: to escape life in the ghetto, to not have to live under the yoke of rabbinical authority, or to better themselves in society. Many Jews considered and still consider the Christian obsession with converting Jews to be a form of antisemitism. Though the Christian fanaticism to convert Jews reached its height in the Middle Ages, it has more or less continued into modern times. In the past, especially the preachers of the Dominican Order took converting Jews to an extreme. A revered Jewish manuscript called the Talmud – containing commentaries and precepts about all facets of social and spiritual life and expanding on Jewish oral tradition (Mishnah) and the Torah – suffered horribly. Allegedly filled with blasphemies about Christianity, it was regularly burned in public during the Middle Ages. Sometimes Jews were even forced to listen to Christian clergy – in their own synagogues – preaching in fervent terms to them about the one and only true faith. There were also public debates (disputations) that lasted for months organized between the Rabbis and representatives of the Church. At these disputations, the Christian side often put forward converted Jews. These converts were frequently religious fanatics; many Jews who converted to Christianity became "more Catholic than the Pope". A lot

Vicente Ferrer, a preacher in the Middle Ages, converted thousands and thousands of Jews to Christianity. A great deal of coercion was used in that period to persuade Jews to convert. The Catholic Church has always considered Vincente Ferrer saintly. This panel was painted by Francesco del Cossa, 1473-1475.

About Jews, Christians, Muslims

Preaching from the pulpit, a priest in Rome attempts to convert the unbelieving Jews.
In the Middle Ages, Jews were often forced to listen to the tirades of priests. This drawing by the Swiss illustrator and painter Hieronymus Hess dates from 1823.

„Die Taufe hat aus ihm keinen Nichtjuden gemacht..."

of animosity existed between Jews who had converted and those who had not. In the history of Islam, there were hardly any incidents of forced conversion. However, this did occur in Iran at the time of the Safawids (sixteenth and seventeenth century), and there were also isolated incidents in Moroccan history. While there were strong feelings of competitiveness, rivalry and hatred in the Christian world between Christians and Jews, Muslims simply looked down on non-Muslims. The word "apes" has always been a common Muslim curse used against Jews; Christians were occasionally called "dogs".

Converting to Judaism

Judaism also has its own tradition of conversion. Particularly in ancient times – in the first three centuries of the Gregorian calendar – Jews and Christians fiercely competed for followers in the countries surrounding the Mediterranean Sea. Exact figures are not known, but millions of people were involved. The Roman Emperor Constantine, who made Christianity the official religion of the Roman Empire at the beginning of the fourth century, prohibited Jews from converting Christians. From then on, it was difficult if not impossible for Jews to continue with this. There were places and periods during the Middle Ages when converting to Judaism was considered a capital offense. As late as the eighteenth century, the Polish Count Valentin Potoski – one of the most famous converts to Judaism – was burnt at the stake for becoming a Jew.

Vicente Ferrer

In the Middle Ages, the Dominican preacher Vicente Ferrer probably had the most success at converting people to Christianity. He was born in Valencia in the year 1350. At the end of the fourteenth and the beginning of the fifteenth century, he traveled all over Europe preaching and converting Cathars, Waldensians (two heretical Christian sects that had many followers in the South of Europe), Jews and Moors (Muslims) to Christianity. He must have been a charismatic speaker. Although it was said that he only spoke the Valencian dialect, even people in Flanders, Northern France, Lombardy, Switzerland, and Genoa hung on his every word. He converted entire Jewish communities in Spain and the South of France in one fell swoop; synagogues were rebuilt into churches. Jewish history books on the Middle Ages describe him as an antisemitic tyrant. However, the Catholic Church considered him saintly. After his death in 1455, he was canonized and today he is still the patron saint of the city of Valencia.

Edgardo Mortara

The story of Edgardo Mortara illustrates just how far forced conversion was sometimes taken. Edgardo grew up in a well-to-do Jewish family in the middle of the nineteenth century in the Italian city of Bologna, which was at that time part of the Papal State. The Catholic nanny of the Mortara family baptized baby Edgardo at a time when he was extremely ill. When the Bolognese authorities heard about this a few years later on, six-year-old Edgardo was removed from his family. As far as the Church was concerned, Jewish parents could not raise a Christian child – the Catholic Church had recognized the baptism of Edgardo. No matter what his parents undertook, they could not get their baptized son back. The struggle over Edgardo's return was a huge scandal, not only in Italy

29 Is there "Islamic antisemitism" nowadays?

There is no doubt that antisemitic myths and legends are presently being widely spread in the Muslim world, especially in the Arab countries. For example, the idea that the Jews were behind the attacks on September 11, 2001 in the United States is believed on a grand scale in many Muslim countries. Via Muslim chat rooms on the Internet, the rumor was widely spread across the world that all the Jews working in the World Trade Center in New York stayed home the day of the attacks, because they knew in advance. For years, the newspapers in Arab countries have been filled with cartoons of bloodthirsty Jews – intent on conquering the world – who manipulate the Americans and are out for Palestinian blood. Should these contemporary antisemitic myths and legends coming from the Muslim world be defined as Islamic antisemitism? Because of the terrorist attacks in the United States in 2001 and the present conflicts in the Middle East, many people feel that there is "a worldwide struggle being fought with Islam". The view that Islam is inherently antisemitic is a component of that feeling. However, "one" Islam does not exist. There are many diverse movements in Islam. Even in the Islamic world itself, there is a range of opinions concerning Israel. Present-day Turkey – also a large Muslim country – has always had and still has good relations with the State of Israel. One must also never forget that down through fourteen centuries of history, the Islamic world was relatively tolerant of the Jewish minority in its midst, especially compared to the Christian world (see

question 23). Because of the climate of religious tolerance in the Ottoman Empire, the persecution of Jews was uncommon, just as it had been in al-Andalus – Medieval Spain during the time of the Muslim rulers.

One should not deny or trivialize the severity and maliciousness of the antisemitic ideas and stereotypes originating in today's Muslim world. However, it is also important to remember that many of these maliciousness stereotypes are easily traced back to antisemitic images that began ages ago in Christian Europe (the Jew as traitor or conspirator, the blood libel myths, etc.). The antisemitism appearing in Muslim countries nowadays was invented in Europe. Therefore, just as it is meaningless to speak of "Christian antisemitism", any reference to "Islamic antisemitism" is also meaningless. Such phrases only "add fuel to the fire" at a politically volatile time in history.

9/11

In the entire Muslim world, from Indonesia to Morocco, many people believe the rumored story that the Israelis or the Mossad (Israeli Secret Service) were behind the attacks on September 11, 2001 in New York and Washington. An extensive survey conducted during the summer of 2002, in nine large Muslim countries (approximately half of the Muslim world), indicated that in eight out of nine countries the majority of people do not believe that Al-Qaeda or other Arab terrorists were responsible for these attacks. By asserting that Jews who worked at the World Trade Center stayed home on that fatal day, many Arab newspapers and magazines furthered this idea. This allegation, especially cruel for family members of American Jews who were victims of this attack, is also a perfect example of the degree of credence given to the antisemitic notion that the Jews are intent on controlling the world (see question 19).

Never Before

The Israeli political-scientist Arieh Stav writes about the daily barrage of antisemitic caricatures and images appearing in the Arab media: "Never before has an entire civilization, spread over 22 countries, constantly, day after day for decades, in hundreds of newspapers, denigrated the image of the Jew and his country. Moreover, if we judge the Arab caricature in terms of virulence, we will find that it exceeds anything that preceded it, including the Nazi caricature…"

Islamophobia

"I am not denying that antisemitism among North-African youngsters has grown due to the conflict in the Middle East and I strongly condemn this. However, I am opposed to any qualification such as Islamic-Arabic antisemitism, because this implies that Islam is inciting hatred toward Jews. This is Islamophobia and in principle this is no different than antisemitism." Tariq Ramadan, philosopher and professor of Islamic studies at the College of Geneva and the University of Fribourg in an interview with the Dutch newspaper *NRC Handelsblad*, February 24, 2004.

Fifty Ques- tions on Antisem- itism

30 thru 33
Countries Connected to the Netherlands

Today's populace of the Netherlands includes a large number of immigrants (and their descendants). Many of them originally came as migrant laborers from Turkey and Morocco in the 1960s and 70s. They were later reunited with family members who were also allowed to emigrate by the Dutch government. Other immigrants to the Netherlands left Surinam (Dutch colony until 1975) and the Caribbean islands of Aruba and the Netherlands Antilles (part of the Kingdom of the Netherlands) for economic and family reasons.

30 Has Morocco had a tolerant history toward Jews?

The present-day Jewish community in Morocco is comprised of around three thousand individuals and is only a shadow of what it once was. The majority of these Jews live in Casablanca, while the rest live in cities such as Fès, Rabat, Marrakech and Tangier. The history of the Jews of Morocco dates back more than two thousand years. There were Jewish settlements even before the country became a province of the Roman Empire. Before the Arab invasion in the eighth century, a number of Berber tribes collectively chose to convert to Judaism. When all the Jews who refused to convert to Christianity had to leave Spain at the end of the fifteenth century, a substantial number of them settled in what is now Morocco. From 1912 until after World War II, the southern part of Morocco was a protectorate of France and the northern part of Spain. These countries, in turn, were protectors of the semi-independent Sultan who ruled Morocco. The pre-war Jewish community in Morocco was comprised of about 250,000 individuals and consisted of different groups: Sephardic Jews with their own language (Judeo-Spanish, also called Ladino), Arabized and Berberized Jews (Arab-speaking), and a small community of European Jews (mainly French-speaking). Before the war, antisemitism played a significantly smaller role in Morocco than in France or other parts of the Arab world. During World War II, Sultan Mohammed V – who later became the King of Morocco – personally protected the Jews of Morocco (see question 34). He was quoted as saying: "I do not know any Jews, I only know Moroccans". Though poverty and poor housing were the primary reasons so many Moroccan Jews still wanted to emigrate after the war, they were also motivated by anti-Jewish riots that claimed dozens of lives. In 1961, King Hassan II finally granted them permission to leave for destinations elsewhere. Large groups then went to Israel, France, and Canada. The Moroccan Jewish community in Israel is one of the largest in the country. Each year, thousands of Jews who emigrated from Morocco visit their former homeland to make the traditional pilgrimage to the graves of the Great Rabbis. The Jews in Morocco were protected as a minority for centuries. However, similar to other Muslim countries (see question 22), they carried the status of second-class citizens (dhimmis). Many Moroccans are justly

(previous page)
The Mellah (Jewish quarter) in the
Moroccan city of Fès before World
War II.

The sultan and later King Moham-
med V of Morocco protected the
Jews in his country during World
War II. As a tribute to him, a forest
bearing his name was planted in
Israel.

proud of the fact that their country has had a relatively tolerant history toward Jews. Historians have praised both predecessors of today's King Mohammed VI – King Mohammed V and King Hassan II – because of the religious tolerance they exhibited. After World War II, the Israelis planted a "Mohammed V Forest" on Mount Hebron in honor of this King. Despite the conflict between Israel and the Palestinians and the fact that Muslim fundamentalist political parties increased in power and influence after the recent elections in 2002, this long tradition of tolerance is still preserved in Morocco today.

Salt

In 1438, the Jews of Fès were forced to settle in a separate Jewish quarter – the Mellah – comparable to the ghettos of Europe (see question 14). The word Mellah comes from the Arab word for salt. Centuries ago, one of the jobs the Jews in Fès performed was salting the heads of executed prisoners or defeated enemies who had been killed before these were displayed in public. Today, the Mellah in Fès is a tourist attraction and Jews no longer live there. Only a museum in a former synagogue in the Mellah and the Jewish cemetery are left to reveal something of the Jewish history of the city of Fès.

Dress Code

Moroccan history has had both its repressive and liberal periods. The Almohads – Muslim Fundamentalists who ruled a part of North Africa and Spain in the twelfth and thirteenth century – were infamous because of the severity of their religious doctrines. A strict dress code was applied for Jews and

Moroccan Jews in the synagogue
of Rabat (1995).

Muslim women. All women had to be veiled in public and Jews were required to wear black jellabas (hooded robes), the exact opposite of the white clothing worn by (religious) Muslims. In addition, Jews who converted to Islam had to wear other kinds of distinguishing clothing such as yellow turbans.

Tolerance
"Islam ... is the Moroccan state's official religion. There are also Jews who are perfectly part of the Moroccan social fabric. The Commander of the Faithful ... is not only commander of Muslims but of the [Jewish and Christian] believers. My grandfather once declared that there were no Jewish citizens, but only Moroccan ones. Morocco is built on tolerance." King Mohammed VI, in an interview with *Time Magazine*, June 20, 2000.

31 Has Turkey had a tolerant history toward Jews?

The Ottoman Sultan Bayezid II (1447-1512) implemented restrictions directed specifically at Jews living under his rule. Yet, he also welcomed Jewish refugees from Spain and Portugal with open arms.

Around twenty thousand Jews presently live in Turkey, mainly in the seaport city of Istanbul. This amount used to be many times greater. There were no less than two million Jews living in Anatolia (the Asian part of Turkey) in the second century. All sorts of artifacts have been found at excavations in and around Turkish seaport cities that shed light on the old and rich Jewish history of the country. For example, the ruins of the synagogue at Sardis, not far from the city of Izmir, disclose that this synagogue was once one of the largest in the world. When Constantinople, the present-day city of Istanbul, fell to the Ottomans on May 29, 1493, the Eastern Orthodox (Christian) Byzantine Empire ended. The Jews of the city did not mourn. For them, the new regime meant progress and more freedom. Fifty years later, however, under the rule of the pious Sultan Bayezid II, religious rulings became stricter again and the synagogues that had originally been tolerated (as well as Christian churches) were closed down. Nonetheless, at that time, large groups of Jewish refugees who had been expelled from Spain and Portugal were still allowed to settle in the Ottoman Empire and build new lives. The Jews in the Ottoman Empire were second-class citizens (dhimmis) for centuries. Stricter in theory than in practice, this status did not keep Jews from regularly being appointed to the court of the Sultan as diplomats or physicians. There has been hardly any actual persecution of Jews in the entire history of the vast Ottoman Empire. However, in the 1930s, there were pogroms against the Jews living in Thrace (the northwestern, European part of Turkey) Many of these Jews then fled to Istanbul. Turkey was also an important escape route for Jewish refugees en route to Palestine (see question 34) during World War II. This tradition of religious tolerance that stems from the Ottoman Empire is also highly regarded in Turkey today, even with the glaring contrast of the autumn 2003 terrorist attack on the Istanbul Synagogue. It is striking that besides its large Sephardic (Oriental-Jewish) community, Istanbul also has a small Ashkenazi community – Jews who originally spoke Yiddish and came from the Crimea.

The Synagogue at Sardis
Around the beginning of the first century, the Synagogue at Sardis was one of the largest and most beautiful in the world. Built about the year 220 B.C.E. and restored in the third century C.E., it was

Sabbathai Zvi (1626-1675) – as the "new Messiah" – had many followers among the Jews living all over Europe. When he was finally forced to convert to Islam, many of his followers turned their backs on him in disillusionment.

A prominent Jew in the Ottoman Empire.

aare afteeldinge van Sabetha Sebi Den genaemden.
herfteller des Joodefchen Rycks.
ty pourtrair de Sabbathai Sevi qui fe dict Restaurateur du Royaume de Juda & Jfrael.

The synagogue at Sardis in Turkey was once one of the largest and most beautiful in the world.

finally destroyed during a great earthquake. A bathhouse and a gymnasium – richly ornamented with mosaic floors and marble walls – were also housed in this huge building. The Synagogue was partially restored in 1970. It is now a popular tourist attraction.

Proclamation of the Sultan

When Sultan Mehmed II ("the conqueror") took control of the city of Constantinople in 1453, he issued a proclamation for all Jews: "… to ascend the site of the Imperial Throne, to dwell in the best of the land, each beneath …his fig tree, with silver and with gold, with wealth and with cattle…." When all the Jews were forced to leave Catholic Spain around fifty years later, the Ottoman Empire became an important safe haven for many Spanish Jews seeking refuge.

Sabbathai Zvi

Sabbathai Zvi – also Sabbatai Sevi – was the most famous Ottoman Jew in history. He was born in 1626 in Smyrna, a Greek seaport city under Ottoman rule. In 1648, he heard "a voice" proclaiming him the new Messiah. Zvi went out into the world and attracted followers everywhere he went, especially because he promised the Jews an end to life in the ghettos. Some historians believe that at least eighty percent of the Jews living in Europe at that time were more or less convinced that Zvi was the Messiah prophesized in the Jewish Bible. Toward the end of his life, however, Zvi was forced by the Sultan to convert to Islam or face death. Though many Jews then turned their backs on him in disillusionment, there are still tens of thousands of descendants of the followers of Zvi, the so-called Dönmeh sect (a Muslim sect), in present-day Turkey.

32 What do we know about the Jews in Surinam?

The Jewish community in Surinam is the oldest existing Jewish community in the Americas. Jewish traders settled there when the (Dutch) Republic of the Seven Provinces conquered the coastal area of present-day Brazil from the Portuguese in 1637. In 1654, when the Portuguese reconquered Brazil, the Jews were expelled as they had been from Portugal earlier on. Some of them subsequently settled on the Surinam River. When the French conquered Cayenne (French Guiana) from the Dutch in 1664, a group of two hundred Portuguese Jews from Cayenne also settled on a tributary of the Surinam River. In 1667, England and the Netherlands signed the Treaty of Breda that also included

The Keizerstraat, a street in Paramaribo, where a synagogue and a mosque stand side-by-side in fellowship.

swapping New Amsterdam (now New York City) for Surinam. In 1669, the Jews in Surinam were granted the right to establish a colony – forty miles outside of the capital city Paramaribo – which would later be called the Jewish Savannah. The Portuguese Jewish community of the Jewish Savannah reached its peak in the middle of eighteenth century. It was then comprised of eight hundred Jewish plantation owners who owned more than one hundred sugarcane plantations and ten thousand slaves. Ashkenazi Jews also settled in Surinam, but they were frequently penniless fortune hunters. The Jewish community in Amsterdam gave them some money and shipped them off to Surinam, under the condition that they would never return home. They were called *despachos* (literally dispatched-ones) and they settled in Paramaribo. When the Jewish Savannah was ravaged by fire in the 1830s, the descendants of the original Sephardic Jews resettled in Paramaribo. Around eight hundred Jews lived in Surinam before World War II. Surinam only absorbed a limited number of European Jewish refugees in the 1930s. The policy of the Dutch government at that time only permitted wealthy Jewish refugees to settle in their western colony. The Jewish community in Surinam today is comprised of a few hundred people. There are still two synagogues in Paramaribo, but one is officially closed and used for other purposes. The Ashkenazi and Sephardic communities merged in 1999. The Keizerstraat in Paramaribo is one of the few streets in the world where a synagogue and a mosque stand side-by-side in fellowship.

The Jewish Savannah

The former Jewish Savannah is situated in the middle of the jungle today. The ruins of one of the oldest synagogues of the Western hemisphere can still be found here. There used to be three cemeteries: two for Jewish plantation owners and their families and one for freed African-Jewish slaves. After a terrible fire in 1832, the Jewish Savannah was abandoned. This area is now on the list of the World Monuments Fund. Once a thriving settlement of Jewish colonists, it is now listed among the 100 most endangered monuments in the world.

33 What do we know about the Jews of Aruba and the Netherlands Antilles?

The Jewish community on the island of Curaçao is about as old as that of Surinam and likewise comprised of the descendants of Sephardic Jews who were forced to flee Brazil (see question 32). In the second half of the seventeenth century, the Jews of Curaçao settled on plantations where coffee, cotton, indigo, citrus fruits, tobacco, and sugarcane were cultivated. The synagogue of Curaçao, Mikvé Israel-Emanuel, dates from 1732 and is the oldest synagogue in the Americas still in use. Jewish merchants in Willemstad, the capital of Curaçao, became wealthy in the eighteenth century trading tropical produce and slaves. When Jews were expelled from the French islands Martinique and Guadeloupe (by order of King Louis XIV) at the end of the seventeenth century, many of them fled to Curaçao. More than two thousand Jews, comprising more than 50 percent of the white population, lived on Curaçao by 1780. The Jews of the island settled around Schottegat Bay (northwest side of Willemstad) in a neighborhood still known as the Jewish quarter. Before World War II, more than twelve hundred Jews lived in the Netherlands Antilles. Today, there are about one hundred Jews living in Curaçao and three hundred in Aruba. The Aruban Jewish community is not as old as the community on Curaçao and is made up almost exclusively of descendants of Ashkenazi Jews who traveled to the Antilles from Amsterdam in the first half of the twentieth century.

Emigration and inter-faith marriages are the cause of the dwindling Jewish communities in the Netherlands Antilles.

The Jews of Statia (St. Eustatius)

The small Caribbean Island of St. Eustatius played an essential role in the American Revolutionary War. As a Netherlands protectorate with a free port (Foreign Trade Zone), it was part of an important transit route for military arms. On November 16, 1776, cannon shots were fired from the island's Fort Orange to welcome a ship sailing under the American flag. St. Eustatius was the first foreign power to recognize the new flag of the United States of America. The British – the opponents of the American colonists who had waged war to gain independence from England – never forgave St. Eustatius. In 1781, they conquered and plundered the island and the Jewish community of St. Eustatius suffered the worst. The British Commander arrested all the Jews on the island, deported thirty Jewish men to the neighboring island of St. Kitts, and sold all their property. He was strongly reprimanded by the British Parliament for his anti-Jewish stance and the harsh actions he undertook on St. Eustatius.

The interior of the synagogue in Willemstad (Curaçao) bears a strong resemblance to the *Snoge*, the Portuguese Synagogue in Amsterdam.

Fifty Questions on Antisemitism

34 thru 39
Related to the
Holocaust or Shoah

34 What is meant by the terms Holocaust and Shoah?

The systematic murder of the European Jews, carried out by the Nazis during World War II (1939-1945), is called the Holocaust or the Shoah. The majority of victims fell in Eastern Europe, especially in Poland and the former Soviet Union. Many Western -European Jews were also killed in the gas chambers of the Nazi extermination camps located in Poland. Not all the Jews were killed in gas chambers; many also died of disease, starvation, and exhaustion due to slave labor. The precise number of victims is not known. Careful estimates vary from five to seven million; a figure of six million Jews is usually adhered to. The National Socialists euphemistically called the murder of the Jews in the countries they had occupied the *Endlösung der Judenfrage* (The Final Solution of the Jewish Question). The Jews were not just ordinary civilian casualties of Hitler's regime; they were a specific

More than a million Jews were murdered in Auschwitz-Birkenau (Poland) during World War II. Auschwitz became the symbol of the Shoah after the war.

Nazi-propaganda, Netherlands (1942): "Yankees, Englishman, Bolsheviks dancing to the music of the Jewish clique."

group targeted by the Nazis for complete extermination. Winston Churchill, prime minister of Britain during World War II, described the mass murder of the Jews as a "crime without a name". The use of the terms Holocaust and Shoah came into fashion after the war. Today the word Holocaust is used the most. Only heard from time to time initially, by the late 1950s, it was being used with increasing regularity. This word – which originates from the Greek word *holokauston* and even appears in Medieval Bibles – means "burnt offering to a heathen god". Though Holocaust was used a few times before World War II to denote an "immense destruction of life" or an "exterminating fire", the word was not commonplace. At other times, it was heard in reference to the mass murder of Christian Armenians at the beginning of the twentieth century; the great earthquake and destruction of San Francisco (1906); vast forest fires or the eruption of devastating volcanoes. In the last decades of the twentieth century, the term Holocaust took on a somewhat broader meaning. Many writers used the word not only to refer to the mass murder of the Jews – in the concentration and extermination camps and by firing squads of the *Einsatzgruppen* (Nazi death squads) – but also to refer to the entire National Socialist policy of persecution directed at Jews and other minorities during the period 1933-1945. Other incidents of genocide are also regularly described as a holocaust, for example, the slaughter of the Tutsis in Rwanda in 1994. Because the original meaning of the word Holocaust is "sacrificial offering", there are objections to its use. The murder of the Jews was not an offering. Therefore, both in Israel and Jewish circles outside of Israel, people usually prefer to speak of the Shoah. Derived from Hebrew, this word means "annihilation" or "annihilating whirlwind" and was already used during the war years to refer to the (annihilation) extermination of the Jewish people by the Nazis in Poland.

One
"Six million Jews were not murdered, one Jew was murdered six million times. Therefore, if you really want to explain what the persecution of the Jews has meant, you would have to write six million biographies of six million individual." Abel J. Herzberg (1893-1989) Dutch-Jewish author of *Between Two Streams: A Diary from Bergen-Belsen*, in an interview with the *Nieuw Israëlietisch Weekblad*, December 1976.

Related to the Holocaust or Shoah

The Netherlands

There were 140,000 Jews living in the Netherlands when Germany invaded on May 10, 1940. More than 10 percent of them were German Jews who had fled to the Netherlands between 1933 and 1940. By the autumn of 1940, the first anti-Jewish decrees had been issued. In 1941, all Jews had to report for registration. In 1942, the German Occupying Forces started confiscating Jewish businesses and property. The Jews were also forced to wear a yellow cloth patch in the shape of a Star of David, so they could be easily identified. The deportations of the Jews began in the summer of that same year. Train transports departed regularly – via Westerbork transit camp located in the east of the Netherlands – to Auschwitz and the other extermination camps in Poland. Of these 140,000 Jews, 107,000 were deported. Only 5,200 of these individuals survived.

Morocco

The southern part of Morocco was a protectorate of France before World War II, and the northern part of Spain. About 190,000 Jews lived in French Morocco during the war: 170,000 Moroccan Jews and 20,000 European Jews who were mostly French-speaking. When the north of France was occupied by Germany in 1940, a pro-German (Vichy) regime was installed in the south of France. In October 1940, the Vichy government issued race laws in all the French territories and protectorates with the aim of excluding Jews from public life. The Sultan of Morocco, Mohammed V, personally arranged that an exception be made for Moroccan Jews. Many European Jews living in French Morocco still ended up in one of the twelve forced-labor and concentration camps scattered around the country, but in the Spanish zone of Morocco, there were no discriminatory measures against Jews implemented. During the war, Casablanca and Tangiers served as important ports of refuge for European Jews. No Jews were deported to the extermination camps in Poland from any part of Morocco. Though the Americans liberated Morocco in 1942, it still took several months before the anti-Jewish laws in French Morocco were revoked. There were anti-Jewish riots in several Moroccan cities after the country's liberation.

The Papal Nuntius (ambassador) in Istanbul, Arch Bishop Angelo Roncalli, dedicated himself to helping Hungarian Jews escape the Nazis. He became Pope John XXIII in 1958.

Turkey

Throughout the greater part of World War II, Turkey remained neutral. At the end of 1943, when there was no longer the threat of a German invasion, Turkey joined the Allied Forces. Turkey served as an important escape route during the Shoah. More than 100,000 Eastern European Jews survived the war by fleeing to Turkey. The Turkish government at that time also actively helped a group of ten thousand Turkish Jews living in the South of France. The Vichy government – which collaborated with Nazi Germany – wanted to hand over this group to the Nazis in 1942 and in 1943. Thanks to the diplomatic intervention of the Turkish government, this was prevented from happening. Some of these Turkish Jews in Vichy France were repatriated to Turkey by train, traveling through Nazi-occupied territory in Italy, Croatia, and Bulgaria. The rest made their way to Spain and Italy. Thanks to American mediation, fifty thousand Rumanian Jews were brought to Istanbul on Turkish boats and then to Palestine in 1944. In addition, the Papal Nuntius (ambassador) in Istanbul, Arch Bishop Angelo Roncalli – who later became Pope John XXIII – dedicated himself to helping Hungarian Jews escape the Nazis. Thanks to his network and with the help of "Certificates of Conversion" prepared by the Church, many Jews did not die. The role Turkey played in saving Jews during the Shoah is an important story that few people have ever heard.

Surinam

During World War II, the Dutch colony of Surinam – located on the northern coast of South America – provided a safe haven to 180 Jewish refugees who were able to flee the Netherlands and Flanders via Portugal. A cemetery in the capital city of Paramaribo – *Jacobusrust* (literally Jacob's rest) – was cleared away so a small village could be built specifically for these refugees. In addition, a huge rally took place in the capital city Paramaribo on December 30, 1942 to protest against the persecution of the Jews in Europe. The Governor, a rabbi, a minister, a Catholic priest, an imam, and a Hindu priest all spoke at this gathering. This group of Jewish refugees left Surinam after the war, but the houses of *Jacobusrust* were not demolished until the 1980s.

The Netherlands Antilles

Once World War II had begun in Europe, the then Governor of the Netherlands Antilles refused to issue visas to Jewish refugees who were in France at that time. This was despite the fact that the Jewish community of the Antilles had collected money for their crossing. However, in 1941 and 1942, transports carrying 160 Jews from Europe were granted permission to land in the Antilles.

35 How are antisemitism and the Shoah related?

The relationship between antisemitism and the Shoah (Holocaust) is not as obvious as people often presume. Certainly, without the Jew-hatred of Hitler and his followers, there would have never been a Shoah. Yet, how essential was antisemitism for the occurrence of the Holocaust? Not every form of antisemitism necessarily leads to violence against Jews, or for that matter, to genocide. An entire library of books has been written about the role antisemitism played in the worldview of Hitler and the National Socialists and about how antisemitism in German led to the murder of the Jews. When the Nazis came to power in Germany in 1933, it was already a well-known fact that they despised the Jews. But that this hatred would actually lead them to attempt the extermination of all of European Jewry was incomprehensible to just about everybody at that time. Though antisemitic feelings ran deep among a portion of the Germany population in the early decades of the twentieth century – certainly when compared to the Netherlands – it was less ingrained than in some other European countries. For example in France and Russia, antisemitic feelings surfaced more frequently and in greater intensity than in Germany. There are two schools of thought among World War II historians about the rela-

Related to the Holocaust or Shoah

tionship of antisemitism and the Shoah: "Intentionalists" versus "Functionalists". The first group contends that Hitler's antisemitism was the motor behind the persecution of the Jews from the outset and that he was out to destroy the Jews from the very start of his political career. According to them, Hitler's extremely antisemitic book, *Mein Kampf* (My Struggle) – written while he was in prison during the 1920s – can be seen as a blueprint for his later political program. This group of historians sees Hitler as both "the" decisive factor and driving force behind the *Endlösung der Judenfrage* (The Final Solution of the Jewish Question). For them, antisemitism – especially in the persona of Hitler – is the most important factor when explaining the Shoah. Members of the second historical school of thought, Functionalists, do not deny that antisemitism in general and Hitler's antisemitism in particular played an important role, but they contend that the relationship between antisemitism and the Shoah is not so straightforward. They argue that "the road to Auschwitz" had many curves in it, which could have ended at any number of different destinations. The Nazi

The entrance gate to the Auschwitz concentration camp, displays the text *Arbeit macht frei* (literally: Labor Sets One Free).

Hitler's book *Mein Kampf* (1925) can be seen as a blueprint for his later political program.

program to create a *Judenrein* (cleansed of Jews) Germany and Europe only led to the extermination camps once other "solutions", such as forced emigration, had failed. The occurrence of Shoah, according to these historians, was more the result of improvisation than of planning. The Nazi decision to exterminate all of Europe's Jews is seen as an end product of the chaos of the Nazi system: a system with many rival groups and conflicting interests that was kept together by an ideologically obsessed leader incapable of planning ahead. What was finally the deciding factor in the decision to create the extermination camps is difficult – if not impossible – to determine today. In retrospect, we observe that relatively few ardent antisemites were needed in Europe to realize the plans to persecute the Jews. What was needed by the Nazis was a conducive political climate where there was little or no protest against the Jews being singled out.

36 Are there differences between the antisemitic ideas of Hitler and earlier forms of Jew-hatred?

Any discussion on the relationship between the Shoah and antisemitism is also partly a discussion about whether Nazism was a direct result of religious and economic antisemitism. Jews had lived in Christian Europe for almost two thousand years and they

An antisemitic campaign poster from the early years of National Socialism in Germany (1920). The drawing is suggesting that a marriage between an "Aryan" woman and a Jewish man will lead to the downfall of Germany, symbolized by the coffin. The swastika was not yet the emblem of Nazi Germany in 1920. Perhaps that explains why this swastika in the upper left-hand corner of this poster is drawn incorrectly.

regularly had to deal with antisemitism and persecution. Yet, never before had an attempt been made to exterminate all of them. Was the antisemitism of Hitler's Germany radically different from other forms of Jew-hatred? The worldview of Hitler was a very personal mixture of religious and racist antisemitism. He saw the struggle of the Aryans against the Jews as a struggle between life and death. Though Hitler himself was outspoken about his opposition to Christianity, he still borrowed ideas from many older Christian antisemitic myths and legends. In the 1920s, during his early years as a politician in Munich, he regularly referred to the Jews as "God-killers". In *Mein Kampf* (1925) he wrote: "Hence today I believe that I am acting in accordance with the will of the Almighty Creator: by defending myself against the Jew, I am fighting for the work of the Lord." Hitler praised Martin Luther's negative attitude toward the Jews, but criticized him as well, because he believed that Luther had spread the "Jewish spirit" among the German people with his translation of the (Latin) Bible into German. Hitler was also heavily influenced by the *Protocols of the Elders of Zion* (see question 17), ultimate proof for him of "the worldwide Jewish conspiracy". He was also extremely impressed by how the *Protocols* had been distributed in the United States by the American car manufacturer Henry Ford. In *Mein Kampf,* he wrote that in the New World (America) "only one great man had gone up against the Jews". Hitler had a portrait of Henry Ford hanging in his office. Hitler saw the Jews first and foremost as a race. In this respect, he was right in step with the racial beliefs of his time. He was deeply convinced that "the mixing of Jewish and Aryan blood" was a danger to the survival of German civilization. He saw the Jews as an inferior people – as an "anti-race": "No, the Jew possesses no culture-creating force of any sort, since the idealism, without which there is no true higher development of man, is not present in him and never was present. Hence his intellect will never have a constructive effect, but will be destructive…" In fact, some of the first laws enacted by the Nazis prohibited Jews and Germans from fraternizing. This sort of racist worldview was not the general norm in those days, but then again, it was not so unusual. What was very unusual was the Nazi success in transforming these sorts of ideas into concrete policies and governmental regulations. The fervor with which Hitler and his National Socialists went about implementing their racial beliefs – turning words into deeds – was one of the major elements of their radicalism.

Goldhagen

In his controversial 1996 book, *Hitler's Willing Executioners*, the American historian Daniel Goldhagen argued that antisemitism in German society in the first half of the twentieth century took on a different form than in other European countries. The antisemitism among "ordinary" Germans was extremer and specifically directed at the destruction of "the enemy". Goldhagen claimed that when Hitler came to power, the antisemitism among the German population was already "pregnant with murder". Many historians argue that without Hitler there would have never been a Holocaust. However, Goldhagen asserted that there would have been "no Holocaust without ordinary Germans…" Perhaps this over-simplified prejudicial statement actually contributed to the surprising success the book had with a large public. Nonetheless, the book also received a lot of criticism from other historians. This criticism was not only directed at the emotional tone of the book, but also at Goldhagen's unrefined, biased and deterministic explanation in answering the question of how the Holocaust could have happened in Germany.

37 Did Hitler also despise other so-called Semites?

The antisemitic ideology of Hitler and the National Socialists was racially motivated. In the Nazi worldview, Arabs – similar to Jews – were Semites and the Semitic race was a pernicious race. At first, Hitler and his followers were barely concerned with the Arab world. However, it is common knowledge that Hitler made a personal remark in 1939 in which he referred to the populace of the Middle East as "painted half-apes that ought to feel the whip". In the 1930s, the National Socialists were opposed to the idea of a Jewish State in Palestine. Only Aryans were entitled to political sovereignty. In the eyes of Germany's Nazis, Jews lacked creativity and idealism, both necessary requirements for building a nation. In 1937, Germany launched a wide-scale propaganda offensive in the Arab world. Britain and France were the controlling powers in the Middle East and North Africa, and Germany needed Arab support against its European adversaries. The German National Socialists tried to convince the Arab population that they were fighting against the same enemy: the British and French (the two colonial powers in the Middle East) and the Jews (who had settled in large numbers in Palestine in the 1920s and 1930s). At the beginning of World War II, many Arab nationalists were convinced that a German victory in Europe would lead also to the end of French and British Colonial Rule in the Middle East. They supported Nazi Germany and Germany supported them. Some Nazi ideologues tried to play down the suggestion that Arabs were also considered Semites. German ambassadors and consuls in the Arab countries even attempted rewriting antisemitic passages in Hitler's book *Mein Kampf* so these passages would be purely anti-Jewish. Arab Nazi parties modeled on the German example sprung up in Egypt, Syria, and Iraq; the Baath political

parties in Syria and Iraq grew out of these Nazi parties. After the fall of Nazi Germany in 1945, the pro-German sentiment in the Arab world never completely vanished. Long after the German defeat, Jews in general, and Zionists in particular, were still portrayed in Arab propaganda as Communists, Bolsheviks, and Soviet agents. In the early 1950s, for example, Gamal Abdel Nasser's regime in Egypt candidly expressed its Nazi-sympathies. In 1964, Nasser, himself, stated in an interview with a German right-wing extremist weekly *Deutsche National-zeitung* that: "…during the war our sympathies were with the Germans" and "…the lie of six million murdered Jews is not taken seriously by anyone." Denial and trivilialization of the Holocaust continues to occur on a grand scale in the Arab world.

The Grand Mufti of Jerusalem

The Grand Mufti, *Haj Amin el-Husseini,* was one of the most important Arab-Palestinian leaders before and during World War II. His struggle against the Jewish settlers and the British Mandate of Palestine (1920 -1946) led him to choose the side of Hitler and the Nazis. He fled to Iraq at the beginning of World War II and supported the Arab resistance fighting the Allied Forces in Iraq, Syria and Lebanon. During the war, he organized Arab broadcasts for Radio Berlin and he helped recruit a Bosnian-Muslim battalion for the German Army in the Balkans. The struggle against the Jews – in Palestine as well as outside its borders – was the focus of Husseini's political ideology. He prevented large groups of Hungarian, Bulgarian, Rumanian, and Italian Jewish refugees from emigrating to Palestine and was therefore instrumental in their demise. Husseini was arrested in France after the war but managed to escape to Egypt, where he remained actively involved in the Arab-Palestinian cause until his death in 1974.

38 Was the Shoah unique?

To what extent the Shoah (Holocaust) was a unique event in history is a question that has been discussed at great length, especially in Israel and other Jewish circles. Must the Shoah be seen as a one-of-a-kind tragedy – unheard of until that time – or was it just one of the many genocides and "crimes against humanity" that have occurred over the course of history? Is it appropriate to speak of an "Armenian Holocaust" or a "Rwandan Holocaust"? Alternatively, must the term Holocaust be exclusively reserved for discussing the persecution and extermination of the Jews during World War II? Questioning the uniqueness of the Shoah is inseparable from the debate over what role antisemitism played in the Holocaust (see questions 35 and 36) and from the question of whether something be can be learnt from the Shoah. In Israel and the United States, Holocaust Education learning modules are part of the core curriculum of many high schools and universities. Jews and non-Jews alike fear that the murder of six million European Jews will be forgotten or trivialized. Or they are afraid that concepts such as Holocaust and Shoah will be used arbitrarily to refer to all sorts of repression and murder. Certainly, there is nothing wrong with comparing the Shoah to other genocides. There are some historians who emphasize that the Shoah was the only time in history when one nation tried to systematically murder every man, woman, and child of a certain ethnic or religious minority as a political goal. Something that did not even occur during the mass murder of the Armenians in Turkey in the early 1920s. The Nazis created a complete bureaucratic apparatus to accomplish their goal. This is the reason these historians see the Shoah as different from all other genocides in history and therefore as absolutely unique. They consequently support reserving the word Holocaust to describe the Shoah and not using it to refer to all other genocides. Still, other historians emphasize how important it is to recognize that each and every instance of genocide is unique. Asking whether the Shoah is particularly unique is immaterial and can even be counter productive. Every catastrophe or act of genocide has its similarities – as well as its differences – with other catastrophes and genocides. This applies to the Shoah as much as it applies to the mass murders of the Tutsis in Rwanda in 1994. It also applies to the many millions who died under the terror of Communism in the Soviet Union and China. Those who stress the uniqueness of the Shoah, according to this group of historians, end up placing the victims and survivors of the Holocaust above those of other genocides, as if ranking these sorts of horrors is even possible.

Even after World War II, it seems that the world community is still unable to prevent new incidents of genocide. In 1994, 800,000 Tutsis were murdered, in just one hundred days, in the African country of Rwanda.

"We may, in the end, conclude that the Holocaust has very unique characteristics among genocides. But to be unique in some ways is not to be unique in all ways. The various perpetrators who became involved in the Final Solution and their decision-making processes were not unique. In fact, I would argue that many of the elements in this were a coming together of quite common factors and ordinary people. That, I think, is very important to recognize if we don't want to place the Holocaust apart as some kind of suprahistorical, mystical event that we cannot fathom and shouldn't even try to understand." American historian Christopher Browning, author of *The Origins of the Final Solution*, from an interview in the American magazine *The Atlantic Monthly*, February 11, 2004.

39 Is Holocaust-denial tolerable?

The murder of six million Jews is the best-documented crime against humanity in history. There is an over abundance of documentation – most of it courtesy of the German government – concerning the planning and execution of this atrocity. There is also a large amount of film and photo material of the liberation of the concentration camps, mass graves being uncovered, and there are countless eyewitness accounts – including many from Holocaust survivors. Nevertheless, there are still those who claim the Holocaust never happened. They argue that the Holocaust is "Jewish propaganda" and a "Jewish lie" and challenge the number of six million victims as being a gross exaggeration. This denial and trivialization of the Holocaust often occurs within a pseudo-scientific framework by Holocaust-deniers ("Negationists") who prefer working under "objective" names such as "Revisionists" or "Historical-Revisionists". Holocaust-denial always has political motives. It is frequently used to attract new followers to the Nazi-ideology (neo-Nazis). Holocaust-denial works in much the same way as other conspiracy theories. As Hitler once said: "… in the big lie there is always a certain force of credibility." Holocaust-denial is punishable by law in many European countries. A ruling in Germany prohibits the dissemination of the *Auschwitzlüge* (The Auschwitz Lie) and Belgium has a law against "Negationism". In the Netherlands, Holocaust-denial falls

There are many Holocaust-deniers ("Negationists") active on the Internet. Efforts on these websites to provide evidence that the Holocaust is Jewish propaganda are used as a weapon in the struggle against "the Jews" and Israel.

under Dutch criminal law: Article 137 c (banning racial slurs or hate-speech), 137 d (banning the incitement of hatred), and 137 e (banning dissemination of discriminatory statements). In the United States, on the other hand, Holocaust-deniers cannot be held accountable under the law. The First Amendment of the U.S. Constitution – which guarantees civil rights such as freedom of speech and the press – prevails over the right to be protected against discrimination. This partly explains why so many English-language websites on the Internet are able to disseminate untruths about the Holocaust. Many European Holocaust-deniers deliberately choose to use American Internet providers so they can spread their message without fear of being prosecuted.

Lies propagated about the Holocaust in the Arab world are primarily used as a weapon in the struggle against Israel. Attempts are made to undermine the *raison d'être* of the State of Israel by seeding doubts about the atrocities committed against the Jews during World War II. In the Arab world, European and American Holocaust-deniers are generally regarded as respected researchers. They are invited to give readings and lectures at universities and appear regularly on Arab television stations claiming that the Holocaust is "Zionistic propaganda". There are hardly any Arab media and websites providing dependable and factual information about Judaism, Jewish history, and the Holocaust.

Fifty Questions on Antisemitism

40 thru 47
About Israel
and the Middle East

40 What is Zionism?

The Austrian journalist Theodor Herzl (1860-1904) is considered the founder of political Zionism. This photo of him was taken in Basel during the first Zionist Congress in 1897.

Zionism is an organized movement of Jews that arose in the late 19th century with the aim of reconstituting a Jewish state in Palestine. Modern Zionism is concerned with the development and support of the State of Israel. The word Zion is derived from the name of the Temple Mount in the city of Jerusalem. There has always been a longing for a Jewish homeland in Jewish tradition. Religious Zionism finally became a concrete political objective at the end of the nineteenth century with the founding of the Zionistic movement by the Austrian journalist Theodor Herzl. The goal of this movement was set down at the first Zionistic Congress in Basel in 1897: "Zionism seeks for the Jewish people a publicly recognized legally secured homeland in Palestine". The Zionistic movement arose in a period of nationalism; new nation states were being established all over the world. For many Jews – but not for all of them – the founding of State of Israel in 1948 was the fulfillment of the Zionistic ideal. The structure created by Herzl and other Zionists was based on four principles: the continuing existence of the Jewish people, the impossibility of Jews assimilating in the Diaspora, the historical right of the Jews to live in the Promised Land, and the rights of others to that land being outweighed by the rights of the Jewish people. While these four ideas are self-evident to those who are in favor of Zionism, critics of Zionism reject this view. The Arab world in general and the Palestinians in particular have always seen the founding of the Jewish State of Israel as an unacceptable occupation of the territory they prefer to call Palestine. The immigration of pioneers to Palestine occurred in several waves. In the 1920s and 1930s, when Palestine was under British rule, hundreds of thousands of European Jews settled there. Shortly after World War II, a major part of European Jewry who had survived the Shoah also emigrated to Palestine. In 1947, the United Nations divided Palestine into a Jewish and an Arab State, a division rejected by Palestinian Arabs. After the declaration of the new independent Jewish State in 1948, Israel was attacked by its Arab neighbors (once British

troops had withdrawn); a war that Israel succeeded in winning.
The "expulsion" and/or "flight" of around 700,000-900,000 Palestinian Arabs continues to be one of the key unresolved issues
in the current conflict between Israel and the Palestinians.
The considerable Jewish exodus from the Muslim world to Israel,
right after the establishment of the new State was also, for the
most part, characterized by expulsion and/or flight. After the War
of Independence in 1948-1949, Israel fought four more wars with
its Arab neighbors. With the support of France and England,
Israel attacked Egypt in 1956 (The Sinai Campaign because
of the nationalization and blockade of the Suez Canal). In 1967,
Israel was attacked by its neighbors (The Six Day War). In 1973,
Egypt and Syria attacked Israel (The Yom Kippur War), recaptur-
ing a small part of the territory they had lost six years earlier.
In 1982, Israel invaded Lebanon in an attempt to end violence and
terrorism on its northern border. Many people see the uprising of

the Palestinian people – the so-called Second Intifada that began in the year 2000 in the Occupied Territories – as the fifth war.

Theodor Herzl

Theodor Herzl (1860-1904) is considered the founder of Zionism. He was born in Budapest, studied law in Vienna, and in the last decade of the nineteenth century became a correspondent in Paris for an Austrian newspaper. The Dreyfus Affair (see question 13) and the wave of antisemitism it provoked in France changed his ideas about what was then known as "The Jewish Question". He no longer believed it was possible for Jews to assimilate into European society. In his 1896 book *Der Judenstaat* (The Jewish State), he appealed for the founding of a Jewish State, preferably in Palestine. Herzl devoted the rest of his life to this objective. He lobbied people such as the German Emperor, the Turkish Sultan, Pope Pius X, the King of Italy, and British and Russian ministers of government. He even lobbied a Russian minister who had been partly responsible for organizing pogroms against Jews.

The Name Palestine

The name Palestine, like the name Israel, is thousands of years old. Derived from the word Philistine, Palestine literally means "the land of the Philistines". It is believed that like the Israelites, the Philistines arrived in the region around twelve hundred years before Christ. They were seafaring raiders who settled along the coast. Similar to what happened to other groups of people throughout history, the Philistines were absorbed by other cultures. Therefore, the Palestinians are not their direct descendants. When the Romans conquered the region, they changed the name of Israel to Palestine. During the Ottoman period – from the sixteenth until the beginning of the twentieth century – the name Palestine was not (officially) used, but informal references remained. After this part of the Ottoman Empire was conquered by the British during World War I, the name Palestine was officially reinstated.

41 What is the relation between Zionism en antisemitism?

The history of Zionism is intertwined in countless ways with the history of antisemitism. For most Jews, the Zionistic ideal was and is inextricably linked to the history of discrimination and antisemitism in Europe. Before World War II, the Zionistic movement was widely supported by European Jews, especially those living in Poland and the Soviet Union who were poor and often persecuted. This was much less the case in the countries of North Africa and the Middle East. The rise of National Socialism and increasing antisemitism in Germany, France, and Eastern Europe in the 1920s and 1930s caused hundreds of thousands of Jews to seek refuge

in Palestine. After the war, a large portion of the Jews who survived the Shoah emigrated to the United States or Israel. A mass migration of Jews from the Muslim world was also set in motion by the founding of the State of Israel in 1948. There had been antisemitic riots and pogroms against the Jews in many Muslim countries in the 1940s. Hundreds of thousands of them fled to Israel or emigrated abroad, often leaving everything behind. Before World War II, more than a million Jews lived in the heart of the Muslim world: North Africa and the Middle East, including Turkey and Iran. Yet, today only some 30,000-40,000 Jews still live scattered across the Arab world – most of them in Turkey and Iran. Comparing only the percentages: the departure of the Jewish population from the Muslim world was more extensive than the demise of the Jewish communities in Europe due to the Holocaust. Zionism can therefore be seen as a reaction to and a result of antisemitism. Yet, in the past decades, Zionism has also provoked a lot of antisemitism. From the Jewish-Israeli perspective, part of the tragedy of the present conflict with the Arab world is that many Arabs have translated their resistance to "Zionism" and (the policies of) Israel into antisemitic slogans and symbols. The antisemitic propaganda that has appeared throughout European history – ranging from Adolf Hiter's *Mein Kampf* to the *Protocols of the Elders of Zion* – is printed nowadays in huge quantities in the Arab world and widely distributed. In the Arab press, antisemitic cartoons that slander Jews are more the norm than the exception. The word Zionist is used as a defamatory word and as a concept it has lost any rational connection that it once had to history or geography. Seldom is a distinction made between the words Jew, Israeli, or Zionist.

42 Is Zionism a form of colonialism?

Especially many Arab politicians and intellectuals believe that Zionism is a form of colonialism. They view the Palestinian struggle as a fight for independence against a colonial oppressor

Nowadays in the Arab media, Israel and Zionism are generally attributed with being blood thirsty and supremely powerful. However, this cartoon from 1967 depicts Zionism as a dwarf being crushed between the hands of two powerful arms: Egypt and Syria. This cartoon appeared in an Egyptian newspaper on the day the Six Day War began. The cartoon is suggesting that a combined Arab front can crush Israel.

Jewish pioneers in Palestine, 1930s.

embodied in Zionism. Zionists are essentially no different to them than the Spanish conquistadors who conquered Latin America or the European colonists who colonized North America, Australia, and parts of Africa and Asia. The equating of Zionism to colonialism occurred as early as 1919 at the first Palestinian National Congress in Jerusalem. The well-known Palestinian writer and activist Edward Said also frequently used this comparison. Although certain aspects of Zionism and colonialism are comparable, other aspects ultimately fall short. It is true that before the establishment of the State of Israel (1948), Jewish Zionists were assisted by the Imperial power that had governed Palestine since 1917, namely the British. However, contrary to the conquistadors or the European colonial rulers of Africa and Asia, the Jewish pioneers did not conquer the country using weapons and force. The Jewish National Fund in Palestine purchased land from Arabs (who usually did not live in Palestine) prior to 1948. Colonial powers, in the past, held on to their colonies because of economic gain or for geo-political and strategic military reasons. However, the Jewish settlers did not come to Israel to "exploit the country" but to invest in it and begin new lives there. Also, Israel does not serve as a stronghold for further conquests in the region. Comparing Zionism to colonialism – where the Israelis are the colonialists and the Palestinians are the colonialized – implies that the Jews have a fatherland to return home to. After all, the French *pieds-noir* in Algeria returned to France after the Algerian Independence in 1962 and the Dutch who settled in the Dutch East Indies returned to the Netherlands after Indonesian Independence in 1948. Those who claim that Zionism is a form of colonialism and therefore all of Israel is occupied – not just the West Bank and Gaza Strip – also imply that all the Jews should just return… though, return to where? Should they go back to Europe, to Iraq, Syria or Egypt? Comparing Zionism to colonialism denies the right of the State of Israel to exist and therefore also the right of Jews to have their own country.

Palestinian Refugees

After the Arab-Israeli War in 1948, 700,000 to 900,000 Palestinians fled the country. As far as many Israelis are concerned, this Palestinian exodus was mainly voluntary. According to most Palestinians, it was an expulsion – a form of ethnic cleansing. In fact, successive Israeli governments have not

allowed these Palestinian refugees to return to their houses and villages. Preventing this return has led to the present-day situation of there being Palestinian refugee camps on the West Bank of the Jordan River, in Gaza, Jordan, Lebanon, and Syria. For the Palestinians, the "right of return" is always one of the most important demands in any Palestinian-Israeli peace negotiations. Israel is unwilling to agree to this because a return of all the Palestinian refugees would put an end to the Jewish character of the State of Israel. If all Palestinians refugees and their descendants were allowed to return to Israel then the Jews in Israel would soon be a minority in their own country.

Occupied Territories

After the Six Day War victory in 1967, Israeli governments that were elected during the 1970s and 1980s gave Jewish colonists permission to build houses and villages in the newly conquered territories. More than 180,000 Jewish colonists settled in the West Bank (overlooking the Jordan River Valley) and several thousand in Gaza. The majority of these people did so for economic reasons, for example, because of the exorbitant prices of housing in the center of Jerusalem. And although in the minority, another sizeable group of colonists also settled in the Occupied Territories because of their religious and political convictions. For them, the Biblical Kingdoms of Judea and Samaria (as they call the West Bank of the Jordan River) are an integral part of the State of Israel. Among the most important reasons given for the bitterness and radicalizing of the Palestinians are these colonists who have settled on what the Palestinians see as their land, as well as the continuing military presence in that area. On more than one occasion, the United Nations Security Council has called upon Israel to end this occupation. The Occupied Territories have long outlived their function as the security-zone(s) they were once meant to be; they are now a heavy financial and military burden for Israel.

Four Wars

"There are four wars: there is a Palestinian war to destroy and replace the state of Israel, which is unjust, and a Palestinian war to establish a state alongside Israel, which is just. And there is an Israeli war to defend the state, which is just, and an Israeli war for Greater Israel, which is unjust. When making particular judgments, you always have to ask who is fighting which war, and what means they have adopted, and whether those means are legitimate for these ends or for any ends. Most of the people attacking Israel or defending it, and most of the people attacking the Palestinians or defending them, don't even begin to do the necessary work." Michael Walzer, professor of social science at the Institute for Advanced Study in Princeton, N.J., author of *Just and Unjust Wars*, in an interview with the American magazine *Imprints*, August 2003.

43 Is Zionism a form of racism?

In 1975, under pressure exerted by the former Soviet Union and the Arab countries, the General Assembly of the United Nations adopted a resolution labeling Zionism as a form of racism. This resolution was rescinded in 1991, even though several Muslim countries along with Cuba, North Korea, and Vietnam voted against repealing it. Nonetheless, in contemporary propaganda directed against Israel, Zionism is still constantly equated with racism and Israel is regularly compared to South Africa at the time of Apartheid. Is Zionism racist and is Israel an Apartheid state? According to Israeli law, every Jew from anywhere in the world has the right to emigrate to Israel (the so-called Law of Return). To address the question "Who is Jewish?" Israel generally applies the Orthodox religious definition of Jewishness. Anyone with a Jewish mother is Jewish, as well as anybody who chooses to convert to Judaism according to the strict Orthodox Jewish rules and rituals (or according to other more recent regulations that apply to conversion recognized and legislated by the Supreme Court of Israel). Jews from more than a hundred countries – all with extremely different ethnic backgrounds – have come to Israel. For example, there is even a sizeable group of "Black Jews" (Falashan) from Ethiopia now living there. Consequently, answering the question "Who is Jewish?" is as much dependent on ancestry as it is on religion. It is therefore incorrect to label Zionism as a form of racism. Apart from this, in all the Arab countries citizenship is also linked to ancestry and it is almost impossible for non-Muslims to be naturalized. Therefore, it is misleading and reckless to label

(Photo top left)
Not all Israelis are Jews. This woman belongs to the Druze community of Israel.
The Druze are an independent religious group in the Middle East. Most of the Druze
live in Israel, Syria, and Lebanon. Though the Druze speak Arabic, especially those
who live in Israel do not consider themselves Arabs.

Druze men, Beit Jann, Israel (1991).

Falashan mother and child. A sizeable group of (Falashan) Jews emigrated from
Ethiopia and now live in Israel.

Zionism as a form of racism while not mentioning the situation in the Muslim countries surrounding Israel.

The separation of ethnic groups (racial segregation) is not legislated in Israel; it is not official the way it was in South Africa at the time of Apartheid or in the American South in the 1960s. These kinds of comparisons are therefore not based on fact. On the other hand, the non-Jewish citizens of Israel – approximately 20 percent of the population (Christians and Arabs) – definitely experience discrimination. They have the status of second-class citizens, for example, they are not allowed to buy land. A United Nations investigation conducted in 1998 listed seventeen laws that were found to be biased against the Arab population of Israel. This non-Jewish population of Israel is composed primarily of descendants of Arabs who did not leave the country during the 1948-1949 War of Independence. The percentage of unemployment among Arab Israelis is almost twice as high as the national average. Voices are heard from the extreme-right of the Israeli political spectrum – especially since the start of the Second Intifada – to expel all Arabs from the country. However, this is not national policy. The life of Palestinian refugees in the West Bank, Gaza Strip and East Jerusalem is even more difficult than that of non-Jewish Israelis, especially when it comes to employment, attending University, going to the hospital or school in Israel, and having to regularly pass through the checkpoints manned by the Israeli Army. These territories were conquered by Israel in 1967 after Syria, Jordan, and Egypt waged war against them. In 2003, approximately 3.7 million Palestinians were living in the Occupied Territories. This population is comprised of refugees and their descendants who fled the country in 1948 and 1949 when the State of Israel was proclaimed, as well as Palestinian families who lived there prior to 1948. There are powerful and legitimate arguments in opposition to the policies of the Israeli government. One of them is that the Israeli government should have never granted Jewish colonists permission to permanently settle in the territories. Another argument is that for far too long, Israel has opposed the establishment of viable Palestinian self-rule. However, even the military occupation of the West Bank, Gaza Strip and East Jerusalem does not justify the comparisons that are sometimes drawn between Israel and the former Apartheid regime of South Africa.

Arab Israelis
Seventy-five percent of approximately one million Arab Israelis are Muslim, more than 13 percent are Christian, and around 10 percent are Druze. Because of the historical ties of the Druzean religious sect to Israel, youngsters from this group – who, for example, actually do not consider themselves an "Arab" minority – are also required to serve in the military along with Jewish youngsters. Though Arab Israelis have the right to vote, many of them stayed home during the last elections. Until recently, the Communist party of Israeli had a considerable following in the Arab community. Almost half of the male Arab population of Israel is employed in construction work.

44 Is the conflict between Israel and the Palestinians a religious conflict?

The conflict between Israel and the Palestinians is essentially a territorial and political matter and not a religious dispute. However, in the past years, religion has been referred to more frequently as a probable cause of this conflict, especially religious fundamentalism. In the Palestinian community, the religious dimension of the conflict now plays a larger role than it did before. There are calls in the mosques for Muslims to wage holy war against the Zionists and "Crusaders" – a term often used to refer to "the West". Radical organizations such as Hamas and the Islamic Jihad, who want to liberate "all of Palestine" and therefore deny Israel's right to exist, are ideologically rooted in Islam and have seen the amount of their followers increase tremendously. The movement in Israel bent on creating "A Greater Israel", including the Occupied Territories, is also primarily inspired by religion. So, in reality, the religious dimension is an important factor in the conflict between Israel and the Palestinians, but in a different way then most people realize. Religion plays an important role in both the Palestinian and the Israeli communities, but this is not meant to imply that these two groups are in the midst of a religious feud. On the

The controls and long waits by the Israeli Army checkpoints of the Occupied Territories are a source of frustration for many Palestinians. Jerusalem, 1990.

"Onward to Al-Aksa!" written on the wall in Arabic for everyone to read. Al-Aska is the name of the Mosque situated on the Temple Mount in Jerusalem, a hill that is sacred to both Muslims and Jews. Al-Aksa is also the most important symbol of the uprisings of the Second Intifada.

contrary, a religious struggle is being waged internally within each group. Hamas and the Islamic Jihad are not only at war with Israel, they are also at war with secular (non-religious) Palestinians – symbolized by the Palestinian Authority. Particularly for them, the war is actually about the character of the future Palestinian State: will it be an Islamic or a secular state? Within Israeli politics, the religious dimension is also essentially a struggle about the character of the State. Israel has never been a secular state because there is no separation of Church and State. Political discussions about marriage, divorce, and education are often futile because the rabbis are basically the controlling authority in all these areas.

Two Wars

"There are two wars here. The one is the Palestinian people's war for its right to free itself from occupation and to establish an independent state. Every decent person should support that cause. The other war is the war of fanatical Islam, from Iran to Gaza and from Lebanon to Kalkilya, to annihilate Israel and to uproot the Jewish people from its homeland. That is a criminal war that every decent person should despise. The bewilderment, confusion and simplification that grips us and the world stems from the fact that Yasser Arafat and his men are waging these two wars as if they were

About Israel and the Middle East

45 Does Israel treat the Palestinians the same as the Nazis treated the Jews?

Not only in the Arab world, but also in debates and discussions in Europe and the United States, comparisons are often made between the fate of the Jews during World War II and the fate of the Palestinians today. "What the Germans did to the Jews, Israel is now doing to the Palestinians" is a remark frequently uttered by people who sympathize with the Palestinian cause. Although the fate of many Palestinians is tragic, this comparison falls short on a number of key points. Israel and the Palestinians are involved in a territorial conflict in which Israel has the military advantage and there seems to be no end in sight. Yet, Israel is not trying to murder all the Palestinians. Such an *Endlösung* or "Final Solution" of the Palestinian question is certainly not the case. In the past three to four years, there have been several thousand Palestinian victims to mourn, but this is different than willfully planning the systematic murder of the Palestinian people. Besides, there have also been many Israeli victims of terrorism. The Israeli Army has taken harsh measures in the past years. Many houses of family members of Palestinians who have carried out (suicide) bombings have been razed to the ground. However, there are no concentration or extermination camps in the West Bank and Gaza Strip. There are no *Einsatzgruppen* (Death Squads) methodically or indiscriminately executing Palestinians only because they are

A contemporary antisemitic theme: Jews depicted as Nazis. This association is the order of the day in the Arabic press.

Al-Sharq Al-Awsat (London), July 11, 2001.

Al-Ba'ath (Syria), March 1, 2000.

Al-Gumhuriyya (Egypt), February 29, 2000.

Sharon kissing Hitler. The association of Jews and Nazis is not only made in the Arab media. This drawing by the Brazilian cartoonist Carlos Latuff circulated on the Internet in 2003.

Palestinians. The conflict between Israel and the Palestinians also has a very different origin then the persecution of the Jews during World War II. The conflict in the Middle East is essentially a struggle about the power over a certain region. Two groups – Israelis and Palestinians – lay claim to the same territory and both defend their claim based on their history and religion. They are unable to agree on possible ways to divide this area, not even after several attempts at negotiation with outside mediation. The National Socialists in Germany, however, had no political or territorial conflict with the Jews of Europe. Racism and antisemitism inspired them and this in turn led to the Holocaust.

Number of Victims (1)

In addition, if one looks at the numbers of victims side-by-side, you see that comparing the Jews to the Nazis is inappropriate. In the first years of the Second Intifada (September 2000-February 2004), according to figures supplied by the Palestinian Red Crescent (Red Cross), more than 2650 Palestinians died. Still, the number of European Jews that perished between 1939 and 1945 in Europe has been estimated at six million. In terms of numbers of victims, the Israeli-Palestinian conflict could be better compared to the Russian occupation of Chechnya and India's military rule of Kashmir. These two areas also have long history of uprisings, oppression, and many (Muslim) victims. There have been extremely large numbers of victims due to the war in Chechnya. According to non-official estimates, more than 100,000 civilians and more than 12,000 Russian soldiers were killed between 1994 and 1996 and between 1999 and 2003. Other sources estimate the amount of fallen Russian soldiers to be as high as 25,000. More than 4,800 civilians perished in Kashmir between 1999 and the end of 2003.

Number of Victims (2)

"In twelve years time, the Nazis killed six million Jews; that is, about 1300 civilian victims per day. If we compare this with Palestinian civilian casualties under the Israeli occupation, we see that Israel killed less people in fifty-four years than the Nazis killed in a week." Joris Luyendijk, a Dutch journalist writing in the daily newspaper *NRC Handelsblad* (January 11, 2003).

46 Is it antisemitic to compare Jews to Nazis?

At pro-Palestinian demonstrations in Europe in the past years, comparisons have often been drawn between Jews and Nazis and between the Star of David (a symbol representing Israel) and the

Dutch illustrator Jos Collignon drew a Palestinian Anne Frank in the Dutch newspaper the *Volkskrant* (October 4, 2002).

Swastika (the symbol of National Socialism). In May 2002, "Sharon = Hitler" and "Sharon > Hitler" was written on countless banners displayed during pro-Palestinian demonstrations. Are these comparisons antisemitic? It is, of course, possible to compare anything and everything to each other, but a legitimate comparison is about similarities and differences. The comparison of Jews and Nazis not only falls short on crucial points, it is the ultimate affront to victims of the Holocaust and their families – likening the victim with their executioner. Moreover, because a distinction is rarely made between Jews and Israelis – Israel collectively representing "the Jew" – such comparisons are antisemitic. Many non-Jews, as well as other people who do not support the policies of the Israeli government experience the comparison – or better the equating – of Jews with Nazis as shocking, hurtful, and obscene. These kinds of comparisons make any further dialogue impossible. As such, they are a sad symbol of the hopelessness of the present situation between Israel and the Palestinians.

Language
"Stereotypes and clichés blur your view of reality. Take a good look at the Israeli media. Almost all media use the language of Ariel Sharon at his worst moments. I keep thinking…this cannot be true. I also

In April 2002, placards equating the policies of the State of Israel with National Socialism were carried at a demonstration against Israel on the Dam Square in the center of Amsterdam. Because of their antisemitic character, signs and banners such as these were confiscated by the Amsterdam police.

About Israel and the Middle East

speak with Palestinians and hear how they perceive us. Many of them speak also the language of their media: provocation, racist attitudes of Israel. It is important to purge language, so we are reminded that not all Israelis are occupiers and not all Palestinians are terrorists." David Grossman, Israeli author and peace activist in the Dutch magazine *De Groene Amsterdammer*, May 2002.

47 Is criticizing Israel antisemitic?

A persistent theme of Arab cartoonists: Israel is only interested in war and does not really want to make peace.

The dove seen by the Jew as dinner and by the Arab as a peace offering. *Al-Ittihad* (Israel), November 27, 2002.

The Jewish snake consuming the dove of peace. (Saudi-Arabia), August 3, 2002.

Israel drawn as the grim reaper – the personification of death – reading aloud a political statement about more planned assassinations (www.Mahjoob.com) August 8, 2001.

Of course, not every criticism of Israel or the political decisions of the Israeli government should be seen as antisemitic. Anyone can and may, for example, reject or criticize the policies of successive Israeli governments regarding the Occupied Territories. This also occurs in Israel itself. However, problems tend to arise because much of the criticism of Israel – not only in the Muslim world but also in the West – questions the fundamental right of a Jewish State to exist and in particular the contemporary State of Israel. This is not only unacceptable to most Israelis, countless numbers of people who live outside of Israel find this unacceptable too. From their standpoint, it seems as if the basic right of Jews themselves to exist is being publicly questioned and this is the reason they consider this antisemitic. It should be possible for people to express differing opinions in writing and to have a pertinent debate about the underlying principles of Zionism. Anti-Zionism is not by definition antisemitic; there are even a few groups of ultra-Orthodox Jews who believe – based on the prophecies of Judaic tradition about the coming of the Messiah – that Israel does not and cannot embody the Zionist ideal. Large groups of Jews living outside of Israel also disapprove of how successive Israel governments have chosen to interpret Zionism. However, on a day-to-day level, a great deal of modern-day anti-Zionism seamlessly turns into antisemitism. And especially when every Jew – no matter where they live in the world – is accused and held responsible for the policies of a government they could not or would not have voted for.

Satire?

"Satirical cartoons beat a quicker path to the subconscious than the psychiatrist's couch. A Norwegian newspaper shows Arafat dressed as a prisoner in a concentration camp, behind barbed wire. Sharon in a black SS-uniform screams at him in German: "Mütze ab! (Hat off!)". A Greek newspaper depicts two Israelis, dressed in the army uniform of the German Wehrmacht, who are slaughtering Palestinians. One says to the other: "Don't feel guilty brother, we didn't spend all that time suffering in Auschwitz without learning something!" The out-and-out politically-correct (French newspaper) Libération dove even deeper into the cesspool of history. Sharon is standing in front of a cross with a hammer and nails in his hand. The caption reads: "No Christmas party for Arafat, but he's welcome to visit for Easter." This is much more than criticism of Israel; this is pure antisemitism." Josef Joffe, commentator and co-publisher of the German weekly *Die Zeit*, February 2004.

Tolerance?

"Were you outraged when Golda Meir claimed there were no Palestinians? You should be equally outraged at the insinuation that Jews are not a nation. Those who denounce Zionism sometimes explain Israel's policies as a product of its Jewish essence. In their view, not only should Israel act differently, it should cease being a Jewish state. Anti-Zionists are prepared to treat Jews equally and fight antisemitic prejudice only if Jews give up their distinctiveness as a nation: Jews as a nation deserve no sympathy and no rights, Jews as individuals are worthy of both…. That argument means that sympathy for Jews is conditional on the political views they espouse. This is hardly an expression of tolerance. It singles Jews out. It is antisemitism." Emanuele Ottolenghi – Fellow in Israel Studies at the Oxford Centre for Hebrew and Jewish Studies and the Middle East Centre at St Antony's College, Oxford – in the British *Guardian* (November 29, 2003).

Fifty Ques- tions on Antisem- itism

48 thru 50
Final Questions

48 How can you tell if antisemitism is on the rise?

Palestinian illustrator Emad Hajjaj points out in his drawing (from *www.Mahjoob.com* on August 24, 2001) that every Palestinian victim results in two new freedom fighters against Israel.

A Palestinian mother, with her children (depicted as suicide bombers) shielded under her wings, stands up to the Israeli attack from the sky. Is this image antisemitic? This drawing by Palestinian illustrator Emad Hajjaj appeared on the Internet (*www.Mahjoob.com*) on August 27, 2001.

It is difficult to conclusively determine if antisemitic ideas are on the rise. Antisemitism is a phenomenon that is especially hard to measure. There is no standard definition of the concept and some people define it more broadly than others (see question 10). Seldom are thorough surveys conducted asking people their ideas and opinions about Jews or inquiring about how much credence they attach to antisemitic prejudices. Besides, in opinion polls on sensitive subjects, people do not always reveal their deepest feelings. They often choose to respond with socially acceptable answers. A method frequently used to determine if antisemitism is on the rise is to look at whether the number of anti-Jewish or antisemitic incidents has increased or decreased. This usually involves non-governmental organizations gathering yearly figures about violent incidents, for example: the defacing of synagogues and headstones in Jewish cemeteries with Nazi symbols (graffiti), threatening Jews on the street, slandering Jews on the Internet, bomb scares directed at Jewish organizations, the attempted arson of buildings belonging to Jewish organizations, etc. Figures such as these can provide an indication of whether antisemitism is on the rise in a society, but they do not reveal much more than this. Experience shows that many incidents are not reported to the police or to organizations that gather and analyze data about these kinds of incidents. Moreover, people who commit acts of violence usually prefer to remain anonymous. This not only makes it more difficult to understand their motives and backgrounds, it can also lead to extremely different interpretations about the acts of violence themselves. One or more perpetrators might even be responsible for an entire series of incidents. And of course, the behavior of a few is not necessarily a good indication of the degree to which certain kinds of ideas have spread among a broad spectrum of the population. The gathering and analyzing of data about antisemitic (and racist) violence is done in the Netherlands by organizations such as the Dutch Monitoring Centre on Racism and Xenophobia (in which the Anne Frank House participates) and the Center for Information and Documentation on Israel (CIDI).

49 What is meant by the "new" antisemitism?

Some people choose to label the significant increase of violent and hateful incidents directed at Jews and Jewish organizations in last few years – also known as "hate crimes" – as the "new" antisemitism. This increase dates from the beginning of the Second Intifada in September 2000 and is especially evident in many European countries. Jewish organizations observe that this increase in violent incidents corresponds with the (negative) shift in public opinion concerning Israel. According to some commentators, for example Avi Becker, secretary-general of the World Jewish Congress: "We have not seen a wave of antisemitism like this one, since World War II." Commentators often explain the increase of anti-Jewish incidents in Europe by blaming Muslim immigrants from the North Africa and the Middle East and the powerful and increasing influence Arab-satellite television exerts on them. Though there is not much discussion in many countries about this increase in anti-Jewish incidents, there is a lot of discussion about how these incidents should be categorized and about the usefulness of a concept such as the "new" antisemitism. Should we actually speak of a "new" wave of antisemitism, or is there only a strong increase of criticism against Israel, which partly gets expressed as antisemitism? Are antisemitic

ПЛЮВІУМЪ

☒ ЗАКОННОЕ ДИТЯ ВИТТОВОЙ ПЛЯСКИ

№ 18.　　С.-Петербургъ, Суббота, 3-го Февраля 1907 года.　　№ 18.

— НУ И ПОДАВАЙТЕ ВАШЪ ГОЛОСЪ ЗА КАДЕТУФЪ!!

ideas prevalent among most Muslims? Does this lead them to turn their empathy for the Palestinian cause into an antipathy for everything Jewish, or do these ideas have a much broader base? And how new (or just how old) is this "new" antisemitism? Many different answers and perspectives exist concerning these questions.

Antisemitic?

"It is difficult to assess the extent to which the new wave of hostility towards Jews, radiating out from the Middle East, is antisemitic. If Jews as Jews align themselves with Israel, publicly and predominantly, then hostility towards Israel is liable to spill over into hostility towards Jews as such. Not that this is justifiable; it is never justifiable to lump all members of a religious or ethnic group together, dissolving the individual into the collective. The belief that all Jews are Zionists, or that all Jews identify with Israel, or that all Jews who identify with Israel support its every action, is false. But while this false belief can reflect an antisemitic canard about Jews forming a cohesive group that acts in unison, it can also be based on a rash generalization from the facts concerning the relationship between Jewry and Israel. A rash generalization, while reprehensible, is not antisemitic." Brian Klug, professor of philosophy at the University of Chicago, in the British magazine *Patterns of Prejudice*, June 2003.

New?

"I have to say that I am not really comfortable with the term "new" antisemitism. As the London Jewish Chronicle put it in an editorial last year, antisemitism is a "light sleeper", easy to rouse. It is also often referred to as a virus, a protean virus which, like disease-causing viruses in the human body, is able to mutate in an opportunistic fashion to defeat whatever defenses or antibodies have been built up against it. It has done so many times, even in post-Holocaust countries whose Jewish population is practically invisible. And it is doing so now." Ruth Ellen Gruber, American journalist in Europe, speaking at a Conference on Antisemitism co-organized by the Anne Frank House in Amsterdam, April 2003.

Safe?

"In Europe, it is not very safe to be a Jew. How could this be? The explanation is not that difficult to find. What we are seeing is pent-up antisemitism, the release – with Israel as the trigger – of a millennium old urge that powerfully infected and shaped European history. What is odd is not the antisemitism of today, but its relative absence during the last half-century. That was the historical anomaly. Holocaust shame kept the demon corked for that half-century. But now the atonement is passed. The genie is out again." Charles Krauthammer, columnist for the American newspaper *The Washington Post*, April 2002.

Exaggerated?

"The alleged recrudescence of antisemitism strikes me as paranoid and exaggerated. By any objective criteria, the modern, acculturated, broadly successful Jew in the western world has never had it so good. We should never be complacent about antisemitism. But at the present time, it is far easier and safer to be a Jew than a Muslim, a black person or an east European asylum seeker." Rabbi David Goldberg in the British newspaper the *Guardian*, January 26, 2002.

50 So, what is finally the essence of antisemitism?

A classic antisemitic theme: Jews depicted as snakes or worms.

Ariel Sharon as a worm. *Al-Riyadh* (Saudi Arabia), September 2, 2001.

"A joke originating from Hungary: During the Six Day War in June 1967, a Hungarian runs into a friend who is beaming. 'Why are you so cheerful?' he asks. The friend replies: 'I've heard the Israelis shot down six Soviet MiGs today.' The next day the friend is even more enthusiastic because 'the Israelis have shot another eight MiGs out of the sky.' But the following day, he looks extremely depressed. 'What's wrong?' the man asks his friend, 'Haven't the Israelis shot down any MiGs today?' His friend replies: 'Yes, of course, but today somebody told me the Israelis are Jews!'

This joke, told about a Hungarian anti-Communist is the story of antisemitism in a nutshell. The antisemites hate the Jews because they are Jews; no matter what they do. Jews are hated because they are rich and ostentatious, or because they are poor and slovenly. They are hated because they played an important role in the Russian Revolution or because other Jews got rich after the fall of Communism. Jews are hated because they allegedly killed Jesus Christ, or then again, because they contaminated Western culture with 'diluted, charitable Christian morals'. Or perhaps it's because they had no fatherland, or they founded the State of Israel? This is the nature of every form of racism and chauvinism. We hate somebody simply because he or she is a Jew, an Arab, a woman, Black, Indian, Muslim, or Hindu. Their personal qualities, actions, achievements are of no interest. If they belong to a despised race, religion, or gender, they are just hated." Uri Avneri, Israeli publicist, in an interview with the Dutch weekly *De Groene Amsterdammer*, January 2004.

Die lernäische Gründerschlange richtet sich auf. Herkules tritt ihr muthig entgegen, um

Glossary

Ancient Times

Period in European history. Antiquity, also referred to as the Ancient World or Classical Antiquity, includes the time of the early Greeks and Romans. This era ended with the fall of the Western Roman Empire (476).

Arab World

Part of the region around the Mediterranean Sea and the Middle East where (predominantly) Arabic is spoken. The great Arab conquests of the seventh century resulted in Islam and the Arabic language being spread across a vast geographic area.

Assyrian Empire

Great and powerful empire in the Middle East from the fourteenth century B.C.E. to the seventh century B.C.E. The northeastern part of present-day Iraq was the heartland of the Assyrian realm.

Austro-Hungarian Empire

An empire of many nations that was organized into one state under the rule of the Imperial House of Habsburg. Austro-Hungary was the heartland of the Habsburg Empire; the capital was Vienna. World War I put an end to the Habsburg Empire.

Babylonian Empire

Empire located between the Tigris and Euphrates Rivers in present-day Iraq. The Babylonians had frequent clashes with the Assyrians. The empire especially flourished during the reign of King Nebuchadnezzar II (605 B.C.E. – 562 B.C.E.).

Capitalism

A social system and economic order characterized by a free market economy. Capitalism has existed since the end of the Middle Ages. Communism, where a government controls the economy, is seen as the opposite of Capitalism.

Colonialism

The occupation of areas outside of Europe by European countries with a specific economic and strategic goal in mind. Colonialism began with the discovery of America. By the beginning of the eighteenth century, many colonies were ruled from abroad by their mother country. Almost all the colonies in the world became independent nations following World War II.

Crusades

Various long expeditions that Western Christian warriors undertook in the Middle Ages to recapture the Holy Places in Palestine from the Muslims. The Crusades lasted from the eleventh century until the thirteenth century and were organized and supported by the Catholic Church.

East Bloc

Group of countries in Central and Eastern Europe formerly under the influence of the Soviet Union. Included among the East Bloc countries – besides the (former) Soviet Union – were Poland, the Czech Republic, Hungary, Slovakia, Rumania and Bulgaria.

Enlightenment

Period in European cultural history (circa eighteenth century). The Enlightenment was characterized by the use of reason and tolerant attitudes. Baruch de Spinoza was considered one of the forerunners of the Enlightenment.

Extermination Camps

Concentration camps the Nazis established in Poland during World War II, especially for carrying out the mass murder of the Jews. Auschwitz-Birkenau, Treblinka, Majdanek, Sobibor en Belzec were among the most notorious extermination camps.

Fifth Column

A clandestine organization at work in another country to further a military invasion or other political objectives.

Freemasons

A private brotherhood with humanistic ideals. Freemasons can be found all over the world. In all different countries, they are autonomously organized into so-called lodges.

French Revolution

Social revolution in France at the end of the eighteenth century (1789-1799). The monarchy was replaced by a republic and democracy. The French Revolution was extremely violent and radical. The reign of Napoleon Bonaparte put an end to this revolution.

Hezbollah

Group of Shiite militants active in Lebanon who oppose Israel. Hezbollah is a major force in Lebanese politics and is supported by Iran. The name of the group means "party of God."

Host

A wafer baked from unleavened flour. Once it is consecrated by a priest, the Host symbolizes the body of Christ. It is handed out to a Catholic congregation during mass in a ceremony called Holy Communion, or the sacrament of the Eucharist.

Inquisition

Meaning inquiry or interrogation (about belief). A tribunal of the Catholic Church to hunt down and punish heretics. The Inquisition began in many European countries in the twelfth century.

Middle Ages

The period in European history between Antiquity and the Renaissance, dating from circa 500 to 1500.

National Socialism

Name of the 1920s political movement in Germany led by Adolf Hitler. Combating Communism and "International Jewry" were central to the ideology of National Socialism.

Netherlands Antilles

Six islands in the Caribbean Sea that are part of the Kingdom of the Netherlands. Aruba (with a separate status as an autonomous country in this Kingdom), Bonaire, Curaçao, Saba, St. Maarten (Dutch part) and St. Eustatius (Statia).

Occupied Territories

The name of the area Israel conquered from its neighbors in 1967. In the year 2004, this area includes: the West Bank of the Jordan River, Gaza, East Jerusalem and the Golan Heights. The term "Occupied Territories" is controversial. Many Israelis prefer the term "Disputed Territories". The majority of the population in these areas is Palestinian.

Ottoman Empire

Name of the Turkish Empire prior to the declaration of a Turkish Republic (1922). The Ottoman Empire was ruled by a dynasty of sultans from the House of Osman. The Empire lasted centuries and encompassed large areas in and around the Mediterranean Sea and the Middle East. The capital city was Constantinople (now Istanbul).

OSCE

Abbreviation for the Organization for Security and Co-operation in Europe. All the European countries as well as the United States, Canada, and the former Soviet Republics in Asia belong to the OSCE. The headquarters of the organization is located in Vienna, Austria.

Persian Empire

Great Middle-Eastern empire of ancient times. The early Persian Empire began in prehistoric times and ended with the Arab conquests in the seventh century. Persia is the former name of Iran. Other Persian Empires arose in the Middle Ages.

Pied-Noirs

Designation for French colonists (and their descendants) in Algeria, which was a French colony until 1962. Many *pied-noirs* returned to France after the independence of Algeria. Literally French for black feet, the name is derived from the black boots the French soldiers wore.

Poor Law

A very controversial law adopted by the British Parliament in 1834. The Poor Law led to all kinds of regulations including that able-bodied poor people would not receive welfare benefits and had to work in poor houses – institutions where people who could not support themselves were required to live.

Renaissance

Cultural period in European history (around 1350 to 1600). Classical Antiquity was rediscovered during the Renaissance. This period is seen as the beginning of the end of the Middle Ages.

Roman Empire

The area controlled by the Romans in Antiquity. The Roman Empire lasted from the third century B.C.E. through the year 476. At the beginning of the Christian era, the Roman Empire included large parts of Europe, the Middle East, and the North of Africa.

Russian Revolution

Revolution in Russia in 1917 and the beginning of the Soviet Union. During this revolution, the Czar was overthrown first (February Revolution) and then the Communists seized power (October Revolution). A bloody civil war was waged in Russia until 1922.

Suez Canal

A (ship) canal in Egypt linking the Mediterranean Sea with the Gulf of Suez and the Red Sea. When President Nasser of Egypt nationalized the Suez Canal in 1956, an international conflict ensued that Israel, France, and Great Britain were drawn into. The intervention of the United Nations resulted in an armistice that prevented an all-out war.

Temple Mount

The place in Jerusalem where Solomon's Temple and later the Temple that was rebuilt by Herod were once located. The Al-Aksa Mosque is also located there. The Temple Mount is considered a Holy Place by Jews, Muslims, and Christians.

Temple of Jerusalem

The Holy Temple (House of God) of the Jewish people that King Solomon commissioned to be built in Jerusalem. It was destroyed by the Babylonian King Nebuchadnezzar in the year 586 B.C.E. The Temple was rebuilt during the reign of Herod the Great in 25 B.C.E. but it was destroyed by the Roman Army in the year 70 C.E. The Wailing Wall, the Holy Place where many Jews come to pray today, is the last remnant of this Temple.

Tanach

The term Tanach is the Jewish name for what Christians call the Old Testament and includes the Torah (Five Books of Moses), Neviim (Prophets) and Ketuvim (Writings).

Twelve Tribes of Israel

The Twelve Tribes of Israel are named after the sons of Jacob: Reuben, Simeon, Levi, Judah, Zebulun, Issachar, Dan, Gad, Asher, Naphtali, Joseph and Benjamin. Each tribe occupied a separate territory in Israel, except the tribe of Levi (who were high priests in the Holy Temple).

World War I

Conflict in Europe and the Middle East fought by the Allies (France, Great Britain, Russia, and later the United States) against Germany and Austro-Hungary. This war lasted from 1914-1918 and resulted in more than ten million people dying and twenty million being wounded.

World War II

Worldwide struggle between the Axis Powers (especially Germany, Japan, Italy) and the Allied Forces (especially the United States, Great Britain, and France). The war lasted from 1939 to 1945. In Europe, the war began with the German invasion of Poland. Millions of European Jews were killed by the Nazis in extermination camps during this war.

Zarathustra

Also known as Zoroaster. Founder of an ancient Persian religion (circa 600 B.C.E.) Many thousands of followers of this religious faith still live in present-day Iran and India.

Acknowledgements

The photographs and illustrations appearing in this book have
been reprinted with the permission of the following organizations
and/or individuals:

Annie Griffith Belt/Corbis/TCS, pp. 5, 152
Beth Hatefutsoth, Photo Archive, Tel Aviv, Israel, pp. 82/83, 84,
    85, 109, 115
Bettmann/Corbis/TCS, pp. 69, 110, 111, 126, 133
Bibliotheca del Galleria Nazionale delle Marche, Urbino, Italy, p. 58
Bibliotheca Rosenthaliana, Collection Joods Historisch Museum
    (Jewish Historical Museum), Amsterdam, The Netherlands,
    p. 88
Bibliothèque de Verdun, France, p. 78
Bibliothèque et Archives Municipales, Besançon, France, p. 57
Bram Budel, p. 161
Bruno Barbey/Magnum, p.112
Bundesarchiv, Koblenz, Germany, pp. 134/135
Carlos Latuff, p. 159
Chris Steele-Perkins/Magnum, p. 8
Collection Anne Frank House, Amsterdam, The Netherlands, p. 129
Collection Joods Historisch Museum, Amsterdam, pp. 32/33, 34
Collection NIOD (Netherlands Institute for War Documentation),
    Amsterdam, pp. 122, 123, 124, 125, 128
Collection KIT (Royal Tropical Institute), Amsterdam, p. 117
Corbis/TCS, p. 39
Daniel H. Wells/Corbis/TCS, p. 157
David Turnly/Corbis/TCS, p. 17
Deutsches Historisches Museum, Berlin, Germany, p. 23
E.M. Lilien/National Photo Collection, Israel, p. 144
E.O. Hoppe/Corbis/TCS, p. 23
Erich Hartmann/Magnum, pp. 40/41
Ferdinando Scianna/Magnum, pp. 4, 5
From the Film: The Passion of the Christ (A Mel Gibson Film,
    USA, 2004), p. 70
From: A. Rubens, A History of the Jewish Costume (London,
    1975), p. 54
From: Eduard Fuchs, Die Juden in der Karikatur [Caricatures
    of Jews] (München [Munich], 1921), pp. 45, 66, 95,
    130, 168, 171
From: Gershom Scholem, Sabbatai Sevi (Princeton, 1973), p. 114
Galleria degli Uffizi (Uffizi Gallery), Florence, Italy, p. 94
Gemeentearchief (GAA - Municipal Archives), Amsterdam, p.73
Harnik Nati/National Photo Collection, Israel, p. 7
Herzog August Bibliothek, Wolfenbüttel, Germany, p. 57
Het Augustijns Instituut, Eindhoven, The Netherlands, p. 92
Hulton Archive/Getty Images, pp. 38, 79
Hulton-Deutsch Collection/Corbis/TCS, p. 69
Jaime Halegua Fotografie, p. 5
Jan Derwig, p. 119
John Springer Collection/Corbis/TCS, p. 69
Jos Collignon, De Volkskrant (Dutch Newspaper), p. 160
Judisches Museum, Frankfurt, Germany, p. 51
Julie-Marthe Cohen, Collection Joods Historisch Museum,
    Amsterdam, p. 54
Kärntner Landesarchis, St. Veit an der Glan, Austria, p. 125
Kevin Frayer/AP Photo, pp. 18/19
Kluger Zoltan/National Photo Collection, Israel, pp. 149, 150
Kunsthistorisches Museum, Wien (Vienna), Austria, p. 29
LAIF/Hollandse Hoogte (Photo Agency), pp. 138/139
Lambeth Palace Library, London, England, p. 53
Library YIVO Institute for Jewish Research, New York, pp. 74/75
Majoob.org, pp. 163, 166
Marius Bremmer, p. 116
MEMRI.org, pp. 67, 105, 147, 151, 159, 163, 169, 170
Micha Bar Am/Magnum, p. 17
Milner Moshe/National Photo Collection, Israel, p. 152
Miriam Philippsborn, p. 23
Museo Nacional del Prado, Madrid, Spain, pp. 26, 87
Owen Franken/Corbis/TCS, p. 9
Passion Play 2000, Oberammergau, Germany, p. 71
Patrick Zachmann/Magnum, p. 6
Patrimonial Nacional, Madrid, p. 51
Picture Library, The British Library, London, p. 57

Sa'ar Ya'acov/National Photo Collection, Israel, p. 153
Sammlung Wolfgang Haney/Catalogue: Abgestempeld,
    [Stamped], p. 45
Shershel Frank/National Photo Collection, Israel, p. 145
Sistine Chapel, Vatican City, Italy, p. 48
Stock Montage/Getty Images (Photo Agency), p. 65
Ted Spiegel/Corbis/TCS, p. 6
The Art Institute of Chicago, p. 91
The Jewish Museum of Turkey, Istanbul, p. 114
The Ministry of Culture and Tourism, Ankara, Turkey, p. 113
The National Gallery, London, pp. 97, 98
The National Library of South Africa, Johannesburg, p. 60
The National Portrait Gallery, London, p. 49
The New York Public Library, New York, pp. 36/37
The Punch Cartoon Library and Archive, London, p. 62
The Saint Michael and Saint Gudula Cathedral, Brussels,
    Belgium, p. 57
The Warburg Institute, London, pp. 57, 92
Thomas Dworzak/Magnum, p. 9
Thorne Anderson/Corbis/TCS, p. 156
Thorvaldsens Museum, København (Copenhagen), Denmark,
    pp. 100/101
Time Life Pictures, p. 112
Universitätsbibliothek Ruprecht-Karls-Universität, Heidelberg,
    Germany, p. 52
Universiteitsmuseum, University of Amsterdam, p. 94
Vereniging Het Spinozahuis (Spinoza House Society),
    's-Gravenhage (The Hague), The Netherlands, p. 35
Victoria & Albert Museum, London, p. 90
Virtual Exhibition, The Center for Holocaust and Genocide
    Studies, University of Minnesota, Minneapolis, USA, p. 68
Wiener Collection, Elias Sourasky Central Library, Tel Aviv
    University, pp. 27, 46, 47, 56, 63, 64, 102

Bibliography

Eposito, John L., *What Everybody Needs to Know About Islam* (Oxford: Oxford University Press, 2002).

Gans, Evelien, *Gojse nijd en joods narcisme* [Goyish Envy and Jewish Narcism] (Amsterdam: Platina, 1994).

Gresh, Alain, and Dominique Vidal, *The New A-Z of the Middle East* (London: I.B. Taurus, 2004).

Hellig, Jocelyn, *The Holocaust and Antisemitism: A Short History* (Oxford: Oneworld Publications, 2003).

Israel, Jonathan I., *De joden van Europa 1550-1750* (Franeker: Uitgeverij van Wijnen, 2003)
[Originally published in English as: European Jewry in the Age of Mercantilism *1550-1750*].

Jansen, Hans/Anne Frank House, *Antisemitisme, een geschiedenis in beeld* [Published in English as:
Anti-Semitism – A History Portrayed] (Amsterdam: Anne Frank House, 1989).

Kertzer, David, *The Popes Against the Jews* (New York: Alfred A. Knopf, 2001).

Lapidus, Ira, *A History of Islamic Societies*, 2nd Edition (Cambridge: Cambridge University Press, 2002).

Laqueur, Walter and Judith Taylor Baumel (eds.), *The Holocaust Encyclopedia*
(New Haven: Yale University Press, 2001).

Lewis, Bernard, *The Jews of Islam* (Princeton: Princeton University Press 1984).

Lewis, Bernard, *Semites and Anti-Semites: An Inquiry into Conflict and Prejudice*
(New York: Norton: 1986).

Lindemann, Albert S., Esau's Tears – *Modern Anti-Semitism and the Rise of the Jews*
(Cambridge: Cambridge University Press, 1997).

Lochery, Neil, *Why Blame Israel?* (London: Icon Books, 2004).

Musaph-Andriesse R.C., *Wat na de Tora kwam, Rabbijnse literatuur van Tora tot Kabbala*
(Baarn: Uitgeverij Ten Have bv, 1985, 3rd revised printing) [Published in English as: *From Torah to
Kabbalah: a basic introduction to the writings of Judaism*].

Oord, Ad van den, *Allochtonen van nu & de oorlog van toen* [Minorities in the Netherlands Today & World
War II] (Den Haag: FORUM / Amsterdam: NIOD, 2004).

Prager, Dennis, and Joseph Telushkin, *Why the Jews? The Reason for Anti-Semitism*
(New York: Simon & Schuster, 2003).

Credits

Text: Jaap Tanja / Anne Frank House

Photo Compilation: Milly Schloss / Anne Frank House

English Translation: Lorraine T. Miller / Epicycles, Amsterdam

Many Thanks to: Ted Musaph, Evelien Gans, Brigitte Boss, Ditske Tanja, Dienke Hondius,
and colleagues at the Anne Frank House

Printing Coordination: Anne Frank House

Design: Beukers Scholma, Haarlem

Printer: Plantijn Casparie, Capelle a/d IJssel

© 2005 Anne Frank House Amsterdam

This publication was made possible by the financial support of the Dutch Ministry of Health, Welfare and Sport

Anne Frank House
PO Box 730
1000 AS Amsterdam
The Netherlands
www.annefrank.org